EUROPEAN SECURITY WITHOUT
THE SOVIET UNION

European Security
without the
Soviet Union

Edited by
Stuart Croft and Phil Williams

FRANK CASS

First published in 1992 in Great Britain by
FRANK CASS & CO. LTD.
Gainsborough House, 11 Gainsborough Road,
London E11 1RS, England

and the United States of America by
FRANK CASS & CO. LTD.
c/o International Specialized Book Services, Inc.
5602 N.E. Hassalo Street, Portland, Oregon 97213

British Library Cataloguing in Publication Data
European Security without the Soviet Union
I. Croft, Stuart II. Williams, Phil
327.1

ISBN 0–7146–3499–9

Library of Congress Cataloging in Publication Data
European security without the Soviet Union / edited by
Stuart Croft and Phil Williams
p.   cm.
Includes bibliographical references.
ISBN 0–7146–3499–9: $34.00
1. Europe – Military policy.   2. Arms control – Europe.
I. Croft, Stuart.   II. Williams, Phil, 1948–   .
UA646.E944   1992
355'.03304–dc20   92–20772
CIP

This group of studies first appeared in a special issue on
'European Security without the Soviet Union' in
Arms Control: Contemporary Security Policy, Vol. 12, No. 3,
published by Frank Cass & Co. Ltd.

Printed in Great Britain by Antony Rowe Ltd.

CONTENTS

Acknowledgement

The editors would like to express their appreciation to Lynn Cohen for her valuable assistance in the preparation of the manuscript.

An Introduction to the Contours of the Debate Over European Security

STUART CROFT and PHIL WILLIAMS

The tectonic shifts in the security landscape in Europe since the summer of 1989 have been bewildering in both their speed and intensity. The disappearance of the Warsaw Pact, the withdrawal of a large proportion of Soviet forces from eastern Europe, the independence and democratization of the central and the east European states, the reunification of Germany, the outbreak of war in Yugoslavia, the progress of western Europe towards the creation of a single market and a political union, and the Paris accords on arms control, conflict prevention, and crisis management measures have contributed to a fundamental change in the landscape of European security. These changes have also created a great deal of conceptual confusion and uncertainty about the future direction of the European security system.[1] This is hardly surprising. Coming as they did at the end of a period in which, as Raymond Aron once remarked, history appeared to have been frozen, developments in Europe have moved with astonishing rapidity. As a result, western European and US policy makers have had to confront some fundamental questions:

– what role should existing institutions play in a future European security arrangement?

– how can strategy be designed when there is no obvious and salient threat to provide a yardstick for planning?

– what is the balance of effort and responsibility between western Europe and the United States in devising and maintaining a post-cold war security system in Europe?

– what is the future role of the United States in European security matters?

Against this background, a conference on *European Security: Towards 2000* was held in September 1991 at the University of Pittsburgh, sponsored by the Strategic Studies Institute of the US Army War College and the Ridgway Center for International Security Studies at the University of Pittsburgh. The aim of the conference was to explore the changing patterns of security in Europe in the aftermath of the revolutions of 1989 in central and eastern Europe and the transformation of the Soviet Union following the failure of the August 1991 coup. Many of the presentations have been revised and updated, and are published in this special issue of *Arms Control*. They deal with some of the most salient issues relating to the future of European security. As a preliminary to these more detailed analyses, we have identified what we believe are the central themes and the main contours of the current debate over European security.

The first concerns the nature of the changes that have taken place and considers whether or not the security environment in Europe will be more or less demanding than it was during the cold war. A crucial aspect of this is the extent to which the future will resemble the Europe of the first half of the twentieth century. Much of this argument has been carried in the pages of *International Security*,[2] and it is clear that there are two broad schools of thought. For the first, Europe will be going forward to the past, and post-cold war Europe will resemble the Europe of the period when ethnic and nationalist tensions dominated the political and security agenda. The other school of thought argues that the Europe of the 1990s is a Europe in which economic integration – at least in the western part of the continent – has superseded traditional national rivalries and made military force largely irrelevant to the relations between the major powers. Few deny, though, that the end of the cold war has brought with it a series of problems that had been contained, suppressed or ignored in the previous 40 years. If there is a common feeling that the euphoria of 1989 was somewhat premature, however, there are major differences about the seriousness of the new threats to security. According to some, the end of the cold war meant an end to the danger of a large-scale war in Europe – and the only real questions are now about the management of ethnic conflicts which, by their nature, tend to be localised. Others argue that the security problems faced in the post-cold war world are in some ways much greater than those of the previous 40 years, and that the geopolitical cocktail of shifting power relationships, greater fluidity, the re-emergence of ethnic and nationalist rivalries, the disintegration of the Soviet Union, and the reunification of Germany provide a mix that is potentially volatile and unstable.

The second theme resolves around the nature of German power and the role Germany is likely to play in the Europe of the future. On this issue too there are sharp differences of perspective and approach. One view here argues that Germany poses no problems for European security, only possible solutions. Germany is seen as the most European and least nationalist of European states, committed to integration and the creation of peaceful interdependencies. A contrasting one is that the only problem likely to arise would come from German insecurity – and the best way to offset this would be to encourage Germany to become a nuclear power. A third view is expressed by those who are concerned about German power and argue that this has to be contained. The debate is further complicated because some feel that Germany is unwilling to face its responsibilities and contribute more fully to out-of-area contingencies, a view that was strengthened by the Gulf conflict. Moreover, even among those who agree that German power poses problems for Europe and that long-run assertiveness will overcome short-term reticence – a process which, they argue, was apparent in German pressure for the recognition of Slovenia and Croatia by the European Community – differences emerge over whether it is a problem of economic power or military equilibrium. Not surprisingly, there are also differences about the appropriate prescriptions, with some seeking a greater role for Germany, others favouring the institutional constraints imposed by the harnessing of German power in the European Community, and others continuing to regard NATO and the US military presence as the crucial constraints on German freedom of action.

The third theme concerns the future of the Commonwealth of Independent States (CIS) as the successor to the Soviet Union. In speculating about possible scenarios for the CIS, one possibility is that the minimalist confederal structure which has emerged will be sustained. Such a structure would allow the states greater autonomy while co-ordinating and managing foreign, defence, and, possibly, economic policies. In this scenario, the CIS will play an active role in international politics, not least because of the dominance of Russia, which is a major player in its own right. The problems facing a confederation of this kind, however, are enormous. Not least is the loss of trained personnel. This is the result of the decline in the economy, but, in turn, is likely to exacerbate that decline. Consequently, some observers see no real alternative to continued disintegration and do not believe that the confederal structure of the CIS can resist the impact of centrifugal forces. The prospect of rivalry and even overt conflict among CIS members is very real. Ukraine's insistence on having its own armed forces – and Russian reaction to this – is indicative of the problems likely to arise as the constituent states become involved in a series of security dilemmas which could fuel conflict.

A fourth theme concerns the stability of central and eastern Europe. There are several sources of instability in the region. These include intermingling nationalism, with its potential for civil strife; great power nationalism or what is sometimes termed hypernationalism, which encourages aggressive policies; lack of civilian, democratic control over the armed forces of the major states in the region; difficulties caused by economic dislocation and the subsequent search for scapegoats; and continued environmental degradation. These problems are likely to be exacerbated by the absence of a security framework. In these circumstances insecurities among the states of the region could prove to be both well-founded and endemic. In this connection, although the Yugoslav crisis is not necessarily a model for the future of central and eastern Europe or the former Soviet Union, it is a salutary warning. Moreover, it has highlighted the difficulties of finding an appropriate response to ethnic strife. Uncertainties about the kinds of action which could contain, limit, or terminate the conflict are worsened by divergence over which institution is best equipped to initiate such measures.

The fifth and closely related theme concerns the role of the institutions in the new European security environment. Some contend that, as the one proven institution, NATO remains the single most important bastion of security; others argue that the Alliance is an anachronism from the cold war, and should either be significantly modified or disbanded. There is no consensus, however, on a replacement for the Alliance. One claimant, as the institution of first resort, is the Conference on Security and Co-operation in Europe (CSCE). But while the CSCE has some support, there is also a recognition of its shortcomings. An institution of some 50 members is somewhat large and unwieldy for dealing with security challenges. The other claimant is the European Community, which is well placed to provide economic aid to central and eastern Europe, as well as the successor states of the Soviet Union. Moreover, as western Europe emerges as a major actor, it will naturally take over security roles which have hitherto been the prerogative of NATO. The Western European Union is seen as one device for achieving this, but it is also viewed as providing a European pillar for NATO. The extent to which these two concepts of WEU are compatible is far from clear. Equally problematic is the nature of the transition from the Atlantic Europe of the cold war to a European Europe which is self-reliant and independent of the United States.

The sixth theme concerns the role of nuclear weapons in the new Europe. The broad consensus is that although nuclear weapons have a continuing role in European security – and there are differences about their precise importance – they are no longer central. This is evident in the Bush initiative of September 1991 to eliminate US ground-based nuclear forces from Europe. Yet there is a distinction between a reduction in the level of nuclear forces and their abolition. Few observers are arguing for the wholesale elimination of nuclear weapons from Europe in the near future. Some residue of extended deterrence, therefore, will remain, although its relevance to potential security problems remains uncertain.

The seventh issue relates to the recognition that out-of-area – or what

Michael Brenner has termed 'out-of-function' – crises will continue to be a problem for an alliance formed to meet a single threat. Whether these challenges emanate from central and eastern Europe or from outside the continent, they are not part of NATO's traditional responsibility. Nevertheless, there is broad agreement that indifference is impossible.

The eighth theme concerns the importance of domestic politics in the future of European security – both in terms of the challenges posed and the ability to meet them. There is a general acknowledgement that domestic factors in central and eastern Europe will determine whether or not the latent potential for instability is transformed into new conflicts. In western Europe domestic politics will help to determine the future security preferences of national governments. The extent to which these preferences are compatible will have considerable impact on the viability of the new security structures.

The final theme relates to the future of the United States' role and presence in Europe. Some contend that US involvement in Europe is essential for the future stability of the continent. For others, however, the United States' role has disappeared along with the disintegration of the Soviet Union. Until these divergencies – which exist in both western Europe and the United States – are hammered out, it is not clear whether there will be simply a change in the internal balance of effort and responsibility in NATO, or a shift in emphasis away from NATO toward more European structures.

A brief introduction of this kind to the contours of the debate on European security cannot hope to be comprehensive in scope, although it does provide a broad framework for thinking about the key issues and arguments. The reader of this special issue will find that many of the articles illuminate the central themes we have identified, and do so in a rich and subtle way.

NOTES

1. There have been some excellent attempts to provide clarification; see especially Adrian Hyde-Price, *European Security Beyond the Cold War*, London: Sage, for the Royal Institute of International Affairs, 1991.
2. See John J. Mearsheimer in 'Back to the Future', *International Security*, Vol.15, No.1, Summer 1990, and the continued debate in the same journal. 'Back to the Future II' (Vol.15, No.2, Fall 1990) and 'Back to the Future III' (Vol.15, No.3).

Nationalism and Instability in the Former Soviet Empire

JACK SNYDER

Some commentators have seen the collapse of the Soviet empire as ushering in a new era of peace and security throughout Europe. Others have argued that the conflicts let loose by the disintegration of the Soviet bloc will soon create nostalgia for the perversely stable cold war stalemate. Which of these predictions will prevail depends largely on the course of nationalism in eastern Europe and the successor states to the Soviet Union, and on the success of efforts by the advanced democracies to influence that course.[1]

Nationalism often seems like an unreasoning force, emotional and impenetrable to argument. Sometimes it is. But often people act politically as nationalists because of a realistic assessment of the costs and benefits of the options available to them.[2] The first step in controlling nationalism in the former Soviet empire is to understand how those costs and benefits might be influenced.

WHAT IS THE PROBLEM?

People define nationalism in different ways, and have different things in mind when they express concern about the dangers of nationalism. In the sphere of international conflict, there are two distinguishable variants of the problem of nationalism.

The first is the problem of the intermingling of different nationalities.[3] One common form of nationalism is the idea that each ethnic group should have its own state. When groups are inextricably intermingled in the same territory, then nationalism drives the groups to fight for the right to set up their own separate state in that territory. The problem becomes international when each group already has its own adjacent state, and those states fight over the territory in which the groups overlap. This is by far the principal type of nationalism problem in the former Soviet empire today. The most virulent disputes – the Serb–Croat and the Armenian–Azeri – are of this type.

The second type of nationalism problem occurs when one ethnic group, already ruling in a powerful state that comprises the vast majority of its ethnic kin, believes that it has the right, obligation, or need to conquer other nationalities, which it regards as inferior and/or implacably threatening.[4] The great power nationalism that contributed to the two World Wars was generally of this type. So far there is very little of this sort of nationalism in evidence in today's Europe.

As Boris Yeltsin's post-coup warning to the breakaway republics suggested, even Russian nationalism nowadays seems to take the form primarily of sensitivity to the fate of Russian minorities in other states, not a desire to dominate other nationalities *per se*. The old-line Communist regime wanted to retain imperial control over non-Russian regions as an end in itself, but Yeltsin's bargaining with the Baltics, for example, focused heavily on the granting of citizenship rights to Russians, not on central control from Moscow. And a Slavophile Russian nationalist like Alexander Solzhenitsyn even argues that Russia must rid itself of the non-Slavic regions in order to save itself.

So when we think about the problem that needs to be solved, it is at present primarily that of intermingled nationalities, each wanting its own state.

CAUSES OF NATIONALISM

It is useful to distinguish among three causes of nationalism: primordial, rational, and manipulative. These may all be present, feeding on each other, in a particular case. But it is important to keep them separate analytically in order to know how to intervene in the processes that promote hypernationalism.

Primordial Nationalism

Some theorists of nationalism argue that the identification of the individual with an ethnic group has been in most times and most places a primary organizing principle of social and political life. Since the dawn of recorded time, groups have called themselves by distinctive names and developed a sense of solidarity on the basis of shared culture, historical memories, and myths of common ancestry. Such groups have typically attached this feeling of solidarity to a particular territory, either the land they currently inhabit or the one where their group originated.[5]

Ethnic consciousness arises initially for a number of psychological reasons, according to primordialist theories. Kinship ties are the most natural and universal way of understanding social relationships and one's own identity in a social context. Ethnic consciousness posits a quasi-kinship relationship with a broad social group sharing some locally distinctive cultural patterns. Not only is this psychologically satisfying; it has the practical benefit of helping to 'inspire or guide collective action' in the community, enhancing the prospects of successful co-operation in joint tasks, including defence against external threats.[6]

The crucial step, according to the primordial theories, occurs when these objective bases for group consciousness are reinforced by myths, handed down for generations, about the group's common past and distinctive character. Typically, these myths revolve around themes such as glorious ancient battles, a past golden age, a return to the promised land, and the sacredness of the 'chosen' people. Actual historical events usually count for less than the myths that are created around them: trivial battles have big effects on social solidarity if they can serve as the kernel for a potent story. Such myths can maintain a group's national consciousness even if its objective common characteristics – like shared language, religion, and territory – are diluted.[7]

Primordialists argue that many contemporary nationalisms have as their core ancient ethnic groups whose national consciousness has been engrained by myths handed down from time immemorial. They acknowledge that subsequent processes of modernization and state-building affected nationalist behaviour by politicizing mass populations, but they argue that the contemporary sense of identity and nationalist attitudes are strongly influenced by traditional myths.[8]

Primordial ethnicity has had less impact on nationalism in western Europe, where modern states formed before mass populations were politically mobilized. The shared experiences and myths producing British and French nationalism took their shape primarily from the shape of the state, rather than from the myths of primordial ethnic groups. As a result, nationalism became more tied to the notion of citizenship within a territory than to the notion of ethnic identity. In some instances primordial ties to Irish, Breton, or other nationalisms remained, or were even strengthened as a reaction to penetration by the broader state culture, but this has been a secondary factor in the political development of the West.

In eastern Europe, by contrast, where the formation of modern states came after popular mobilization, national consciousness was shaped more by primordial myths.[9] Because of the intermixture of populations, ethnic boundaries did not conform to state boundaries. Moreover, because primordial ethnic groups were already politically engaged while states were still weak, it was often impossible to create a new nation-state consciousness in lieu of the primordial loyalties. Much of the hypernationalism of eastern European politics before the two World Wars was caused by the fatal juxtaposition of longstanding ethnic myths with mobilized, intermixed populations. That is, the problem was the interactive effect of primordial and modernizing forces. The upheavals of populations during and after World War II somewhat reduced, but hardly eliminated the mismatch between state boundaries and national consciousness in that region.

Some of the most virulent nationalisms arising from Communism's wreckage have a primordial character. Serbian and Armenian militancy *vis-à-vis* their ancient ethnic enemies, for example, is fuelled by the desire to hold ancestral lands in Kosovo and Nagorno-Karabakh and by myths of ancient battles, massacres, and golden-age empires. Likewise, Azerbaijani intellectuals are more interested in detailing the injustices of past millenia than in exploring practical conflict-management strategies for today's problems.

Such intense, primordial conflicts interact with a number of contemporary factors – the weakening of the repressive hand of the central state, zero-sum economic competition in hard times, and the exploitation of nationalism by political elites. To mitigate these modern complications might reduce the effects of primordial conflicts. It seemed a misdiagnosis, however, when Moscow's liberal reformers argued that the economic success of *perestroika* would make such primordial tensions vanish.

As intractable as these primordial conflicts may be, they have in themselves only a limited potential for disrupting the broader security of Europe. Primordial nationalism has inherently limited aims: the reconquest of lost lands and the reincorporation of displaced brethren. Unless admixed with other elements, it is not a recipe for open-ended conquest. Moreover, most of the potent primordial nationalisms of the former Soviet empire are found in relatively small groups which lack great geopolitical significance or power potential. Their ability to cause wider trouble will hinge on whether larger states intervene in their squabbles. Antidotes should probably focus less on solving these disputes than on sealing off their effects from wider political relationships.

The bigger potential nation-states – Ukraine, Russia, and Poland – so far lack the intense grievances that would trigger primordial ethnic feuds with other groups. However, the problem of Russian minorities in the non-Russian states in the Commonwealth of Independent States (CIS), could create such an issue. Fortunately, primordial ethnic consciousness is not especially great in the eastern Ukrainian regions where Russians and Ukrainians are intermingled.[10] Theories of nationalism that stress modern, rather than primordial variables, seem better suited for the study of these more consequential cases.

Rational Nationalism

Balkan-style hypernationalism seems anything but rational from the vantage point of a North American, liberal sensibility. Even an objective journalist like Robert MacNeill has been reduced to head-shaking puzzlement and exasperation when interviewing Serbs and Croats on their dispute. But when other routes to an individual's economic and security goals are blocked, nationalistic political action may make perfect sense.

War and State-building

The need for collective self-defence is a particularly strong, rational incentive for nationalism. As Charles Tilly contends, war made the state, the state made war, and they both together made nationalism.[11]

Experiencing a common external threat often convinces people living together in a state that they share a common fate. Instead of defining their main interests and loyalties in terms of cleavages within society, they do so in terms of enmities between societies. Nationalism is spurred not only during war itself, but by international crises, by hostile encirclements, and through the searing memories of past wars.[12]

Some theorists argue not only that military threats spur nationalism, but also that the systemic effects of international anarchy set up an echo chamber that amplifies nationalistic sentiments into hypernationalism. In this view, potential threats from one state may spur nationalistic reactions in another. These reactions in turn may heighten the first state's sense of threat, and hence its sentiment of nationalism, touching off an uncontrollable spiral into hypernationalism on both sides.

In this realist view, the most nationalist states should be those that occupy the most vulnerable positions in the international system. Nationalism has been especially prominent in German history, for example, because of Germany's vulnerable geographical position in central Europe and because Germany's dynamism has necessarily provoked the fears and hostility of its neighbours. Thus the encircling alliances provoked by Germany's aggressive diplomacy before 1914 confirmed the self-fulfilling prophecies of nationalist statesmen and ideologues: the outside world *was* indeed hostile to German national aims, and the fate of every German depended on his uniting to combat these implacable foes.

Today the likelihood that international conflict will spur nationalism among Europe's great powers is fairly low. Moscow's 'new thinkers' understand that the Soviet Union provoked a hostile encirclement through its past belligerent policies. Despite the Soviet Union's geopolitical retreats, they see the threat to Russian security from other great powers as quite low. 'Old thinkers' among the Communist Party bureaucrats and the military argued a new version of the stab-in-the-back myth: Gorbachev's liberals traitorously abandoned the Soviet Union's security buffer in Europe, thus allowing Germany to reconstitute its power in league with the ring-leader of imperialism, the United States.[13] But such arguments failed to touch a strong chord with Great Russian nationalist sentiment, which seems more inclined to retreat into isolationism in order to be rid of the thankless burdens of empire. As some Western commentators note, however, the insecurities provoked by the new, more fluid, multipolar distribution of power in Europe create an inherent risk of stimulating nationalist thinking.

In order to avoid a backlash of belligerent Russian nationalism, the West attempted to allay Soviet fears over the reunification of Germany. The London Declaration, stressing NATO's benign intentions toward the Soviet Union, was a conscious attempt to help Gorbachev against stab-in-the-back criticism.[14] Further steps can be taken to underscore this message, including the strengthening of pan-European security structures, as in the Conference on Security and Co-operation in Europe, which Moscow desires. Arms control, as well as unilateral decisions to avoid offensive military postures, can also help to dampen nationalism by reducing the atmosphere of threat.

If threats of East–West war are not worrying as a source of nationalism, East–East security threats are. One of the prime motivators of the Serb–Croat fighting is the fear that nationals of the one group might be physically exterminated if left as minorities in a state dominated by the other. It happened during World War II, so they reason that it might happen again. Consequently, the costs of fighting look acceptable when compared with the costs of failing to resist incorporation into another's state.

If the break-up of the Yugoslav state has triggered aggression out of these security fears, will this happen as a result of the break-up of the Soviet Union as well? New states with ethnically intertwined populations will have vastly unequal military resources. They may be worried that other states will disregard minority rights and use their military power to solve nationality disputes unilaterally. Whether this is true or not, each new state will have to worry that it might be true, and so it has an incentive to embark on competitive military preparations just in case. If they all act on this logic, the contemporary period of state formation in the East may recapitulate the pattern of state formation in the West, with its pattern of reciprocal reinforcement between war and nationalism.

This may indeed occur in some instances, such as between the Azeris and the Armenians, where primordial enmities are already strong. But as yet there seems to be little sign of this in the relationships between larger states, such as Russia and Ukraine. The Ukrainians have been using the nuclear weapons on their soil as a diplomatic bargaining card in their relations with the Russians, and they initially announced their intention of creating an army of several hundred thousand troops. But economic constraints and diplomatic reservations expressed by other nations have led Ukraine to scale down its military goals to a modest 90,000 troops, as of December 1991.[15]

In short, nationalism for the purpose of military mobilization may be a rational response to conditions of international threat, but those conditions seem to be strong enough to spur hypernationalism only in a few locations in the former Soviet empire.

Economic Incentives

The collapse of the Soviet empire is creating two kinds of rational economic spur to nationalism. The first is simply that the command economy run from Moscow has collapsed, and the central authorities have put nothing in its place. Peoples and governments in the republics realize that, to avoid chaos, they cannot wait for viable reforms to be handed down from the politically-crippled, central government. Nor can they count on some new, recentralized system to emerge from complex, slow bargaining among a variety of independent actors with conflicting interests. They have concluded that economic decisions must be taken by the only remaining levels of government that still function, and this means, by default, the republics. What looks like irrational nationalism – banning the export of goods, moving towards a local currency – may be simply the short-term rational reaction to the co-ordination problems of a multi-person 'prisoner's dilemma'.

A second economic spur to nationalism may come from the differential effects of market reform on national groups. Indeed, one of the major theories of the origins of modern nationalism stresses the role of economic modernization and marketization. According to Ernest Gellner, in pre-industrial societies, homogeneity of language and culture were unnecessary for the political and economic functioning of society. Elites, often with cosmopolitan cultures, ruled over and extracted an economic surplus from an agrarian population, often embodying a mixture of local dialects and cultures. This culture heterogeneity affected politics and economics very little, since the efficiency of local production and the extraction of resources were not closely tied to culture. Mass ethnic consciousness played a relatively small role in political life.[16]

With the arrival of industrial society, however, the co-ordination of economic activities within an extensive division of labour required greater linguistic and cultural homogeneity. For specialized producers to mesh their efforts smoothly, a common understanding of cultural signals, including but not limited to a common language, became essential. Which culture would provide the lingua franca within a given political unit became a crucial issue for the 'life chances' of individual members of the industrializing society. Wherever industrialization occurred, ethnic groups vied for the advantage of supplying the dominant culture that would grease the wheels of economic activity, and nationalism intensified.

Recent events suggest that this thesis retains its force. In Quebec, French nationalism has permitted the ascendancy of a new French-speaking economic elite. In what was the Soviet Union, the ethnic groups that are the most advanced economically, those in the Baltic area and the Caucasus, are the most nationalist. Conversely, the relatively unmobilized, traditional societies of Central Asia have been slow to develop a coherent, politicized national consciousness.

If industrial society is, in general, a cause of nationalism, the transition to a modern market economy is a particularly intense cause of it. The introduction of markets normally produces a sharp increase in inequality and is likely to have a differential effect on the fortunes of different ethnic groups. Since economic modernization also heightens the economic importance of language and culture, nationalist conflict is especially intense during such a transition.[17] Losers in the process of market reform, such as the downwardly-mobile artisans of Wilhelmine Germany, are easy to recruit for folkish nationalist movements, which demand a return to a golden age of regulated economics and purported social solidarity.[18]

Eventually the economic and social stresses of the transition are overcome, inequality is normally reduced, and minorities are often assimilated by the dominant culture or compensated by it. National sentiment and conflict remain, but are typically less intense than during the initial introduction of modern markets.[19]

The entire former Eastern bloc is on the verge of a transition to a market economy. In several states this may increase inequalities between ethnic groups whose differing skill endowments and cultural character-istics give them differing abilities to exploit market opportunities. Slovenes and Croats are poised to benefit from the expansion of market opportunities, whereas other Yugoslav national groups may not be. Czechs and Slovaks may face different market chances for geographical as well as cultural reasons. In the CIS, the introduction of world market prices for energy and raw materials would benefit Russia at the expense of the other states.

To avert a nationalist explosion, the blow from the introduction of markets must be cushioned. This can be done both by expanding the total size of the economic pie and by distributing its pieces more equitably. Influxes of foreign capital would ease the transition to a market system for all groups. At the same time, the workings of the market should be regulated to buffer those who bear the greatest burdens of adjustment.

MANIPULATIVE NATIONALISM

Military competition and economic change not only provide rational incentives for nationalist political behaviour, they also heighten incentives for elites to create nationalist myths. Military and economic pressures increase demands on the state and make governing more difficult. Weak, hard-pressed, or newly-emerging states may try to exploit nationalist sentiment in order to strengthen their hand in dealing with these challenges. As a by-product, they may turn nationalism into hypernationalism. Likewise, non-state intellectuals in such conditions may seize the opportunity to fan nationalist sentiments in order to establish a state that they can rule.

This has been occurring throughout the Balkans and the former Soviet periphery. Communist and former Communist rulers, in particular, have been eager to take on the mantle of nationalism in order to gain a renewed source of legitimacy. Often this has touched off a spiral of competition between old elites and new anti-Communist groups to try to prove who is the most purely nationalist. Such competitions have deepened the nationalist tendencies in Serbia, Azerbaijan, and elsewhere.

The wider international community might take several steps to reduce the attractiveness of nationalist, demagogic strategies to these states. First, it can proceed with arms control and pan-European security efforts to reduce the persuasiveness of threat-inflating rhetoric. Second, it can provide incentives and resources to facilitate non-nationalistic strategies of rule. For example, if Hungary and Romania receive substantial benefits from integrating their economies with those of the European Community, their governments will be able to substitute internationalist appeals for nationalist rhetoric in rallying domestic support for their programmes. To some extent, this might happen automatically, as a natural political result of the 'invisible hand' of economic incentives. However, Western states should also use the 'visible hand' of explicit linkage, tying credits and trade concessions to the satisfactory treatment of ethnic minorities, respect for individual human rights, the institutionalization of democratic reforms, the curtailment of inflammatory nationalist propaganda, and the banning of nationalistic history texts in schools. The European Bank for Reconstruction and Development, for example, deferred Romanian eligibility after the government's use of miners to suppress legitimate political expression. Minority treatment and individual rights are explicit criteria considered by the EC and the

EBRD in deciding on further ties with eastern states.[20]

CONCLUSION

Nationalism poses the most acute threat to domestic and international security in the region of the former Soviet empire. Though a few of these nationalist clashes are deeply entrenched in primordial enmity, most potential nationalisms in the region are of a more malleable type. They respond to rational changes in economic and security incentives, as well as the manipulative strategies of elites. Consequently, there is a reasonable chance that the virulence of these nationalisms can be mitigated by the policies of outside powers that affect those incentives. Promoting a stable security environment, buffering populations from the rigors of economic change, and linking economic aid to the benign treatment of minorities should help to serve these ends.

NOTES

1. Sean Lynn-Jones (ed.), *The Cold War and After* (Cambridge: MIT, 1991).
2. Ronald Rogowski, 'Causes and Varieties of Nationalism: A Rationalist Account', in: Edward Tiryakian and R. Rogowski, *New Nationalisms of the Developed West* (Boston: Allen & Unwin, 1985).
3. For an example, see Myron Weiner, 'The Macedonian Syndrome', *World Politics*, Vol.23, No.4, July 1971, pp. 655–83.
4. For example, Carlton Hayes, *The Historical Evolution of Modern Nationalism* (New York: Russell & Russell, 1931).
5. Anthony D. Smith, *The Ethnic Origins of Nations* (Oxford: Blackwell, 1986), p.32.
6. Ibid., pp.24–5.
7. Ibid., p.28.
8. Ibid., Ch.6–9.
9. Ibid., pp.135–7, citing Hans Kohn, *The Idea of Nationalism* (New York: Collier-Macmillan, 2nd ed., 1967), Ch.5.
10. For background, see Rasma Karklins, *Ethnic Relations in the USSR* (Boston: Allen & Unwin, 1986); Alexander Motyl, *Sovietology, Rationality, Nationality* (New York: Columbia, 1990); John Armstrong, *Ukrainian Nationalism* (Littleton, Co: Ukrainian Academic Press, 3rd ed., 1990).
11. Charles Tilly, *Coercion, Capital, and European States* (Oxford: Blackwell, 1990).
12. For general discussions, see Joseph Rothschild, *Ethnopolitics* (New York: Columbia, 1981), Ch.6, and Smith, op. cit., pp.37–41. For some examples, see Boyd C. Shafer, *Faces of Nationalism* (New York: Harcourt Brace Jovanovich, 1972), Ch.5, on the Napoleonic period; Kingsley Martin, *The Triumph of Lord Palmerston: a Study of Public Opinion in England before the Crimean War* (London: Hutchinson, revised ed., 1963); and W. G. Beasley, *The Meiji Restoration* (Stanford: Stanford University Press, 1972).
13. See, for example, speeches by Yegor Ligachev and others at the Communist Party Congress, reported and excerpted in Bill Keller, 'Soviet Hardliner Assails Gorbachev on His Leadership', *New York Times*, 4 July 1990, pp.1, 6.
14. *New York Times*, 6 July 1990, p.1.
15. Kathleen Mihalisko, 'Laying the Foundation for the Armed Forces of the Ukraine',

Report on the USSR, Radio Liberty, 8 November 1991, pp.19–22; Francis X. Clines, 'Ukraine Reduces Plans for an Army', *New York Times*, 1 December 1991, p.1.

16. Ernest Gellner, *Nations and Nationalism* (Ithaca: Cornell University Press, 1983).
17. Ibid., pp.73–4, 111.
18. Woodruff Smith, *Ideological Origins of Nazi Imperialism* (New York: Oxford University Press, 1986); Eley, *Reshaping the German Right* (New Haven: Yale University Press, 1980); Hans-Ulrich Wehler, *The German Empire, 1871–1918* (Leamington Spa: Berg, 1985).
19. Gellner, op. cit., pp.40, 121.
20. On the EBRD, see *New York Times*, 30 May 1990, p.14. It may be worth recalling that the Minorities Protection Treaties of 1919 failed because the League of Nations had inadequate enforcement powers and because Germany and Hungary used the treaties as an offensive weapon to press their irredentist claims against Poland and Romania. After World War II, the United Nations sought to secure minority groups' rights indirectly, through agreements to respect individuals' rights. See Rothschild, op. cit., pp.176–7.

NATO Reborn

JAMES EBERLE

For more than 40 years, NATO has had a clear and visible primary purpose – the defence of western Europe against the threat of military aggression by the Soviet Union and its Warsaw Pact allies. NATO's aim has been to break down the post-Second World War barriers that had been erected between East and West. It has also served a number of other purposes, not least by providing in the political field a strong and vital link in security policy between the United States and western Europe; and in the military field by building the habit of international co-operation amongst the armed forces of 16 countries to a degree which has not been achieved in almost any other field. Under such conditions, military action by one member state against another becomes difficult to conceive and to execute.

Now the threat of military aggression by the Soviet Union or Russia has effectively disappeared; at least for the present. The Warsaw Pact is no more. Eastern Europe has thrown off the dead hand of Communist rule. The 'iron curtain' has been torn down. If NATO has thus achieved its primary purpose, then the question has to be asked 'is this the end of NATO?' If it is not, and there is a 'new NATO' waiting to be born, then what is its new purpose and how can it best be fulfilled? We cannot separate consideration of these issues from even more fundamental questions about the effectiveness of military power, and the role of alliances in the 'New World Order' which we are attempting to fashion.

THE UTILITY OF MILITARY POWER

It has been my contention for a number of years that the utility of military power is changing. The use of force is becoming increasingly less effective as a means of successfully achieving political goals. At the nuclear level it has been clear for a long time that these weapons were almost unusable, because they have become too powerful. To initiate nuclear war would entail not only destroying the enemy, but also risking the destruction of one's own country; and perhaps, through escalation in a strategic exchange, even ending civilization in the world as we now know it. Nevertheless, the threat of their use has remained sufficiently credible to provide the deterrence of the ultimate sanction. At the conventional level, I have argued that the potential cost of conducting large-scale conventional operations, bearing in mind the destructive capability of modern weapons and the sophistication of the infrastructure of a modern economy against which they might be directed, is so great that a major conventional war is becoming no longer an effective option for the settlement of international disputes.

It may be useful briefly to assess this hypothesis against recent events in eastern Europe, the Middle East, the Soviet Union and Yugoslavia. In eastern Europe, real and fundamental political change was achieved, almost without violence, by means of 'peaceful people power'. In the Soviet Union, despite support for the coup being given by the Minister of Defence, Marshal Yazov, and a number of senior generals, and tanks being deployed on the streets of Moscow, the armed forces played a relatively small part in either the coup or its suppression; although the symbolism provided by the small number of armoured vehicles that deployed to defend Mr Yeltsin and the Russian Parliament was important.

In the Middle East, the allied forces inflicted a crushing defeat upon the Iraqi armed forces occupying Kuwait, in the largest scale military operation that has been mounted since the end of the Second World War. The United Nations' stated aim of restoring the legitimate government of Kuwait was achieved with minimal allied losses. Very heavy costs were extracted from the Iraqi side, both to their armed forces and to the structure of their civil society, costs which may not unreasonably be seen to be disproportionate to the scale of the original aggression. The operation was not, however, without cost on the allied side. Apart from the obvious costs of mounting the operation and of the reconstruction of Kuwait, there has been heavy and widespread pollution from the torching of the oil wells and the destruction of the refineries, the West has been drawn in to the issue of the independence of the Kurds, and there has been a strengthening of fundamentalism in some Arab countries. But perhaps the greatest cost is carried in the perception that, although the allies had a great and glorious victory in battle, the war has not been won; and that although the war has changed the problem, it has not solved it. Saddam Hussein is still in power in Iraq. He continues to perpetrate horrifying abuses of human rights upon his own people and continues to defy the United Nations. Despite some progress in the Middle East Peace Conference, lasting peace and stability in the region continues to resemble a dream. Once again, the use of military force, this time with great military success, has been ineffective in producing the wider political outcome that was desired.

In Yugoslavia, despite all efforts by the European Community to obtain an effective cease-fire, violence in Croatia steadily escalated to civil war. Nevertheless, this escalation has been accompanied by verbal recognition from both sides that a solution cannot be achieved by military means. The plight of the elderly, the injuries to children and the damage to part of Europe's cultural heritage, as in Dubrovnik, which have been vividly illustrated on television screens around the world, must surely re-enforce the view that war can no longer be an effective and acceptable means of achieving political change.

This is, of course, not to say that military power is no longer an important factor in international relations; nor yet as a factor in national politics. I do, however, believe that the way in which military power can be used effectively has changed, and continues to change. Politico-military factors are now relatively less important than those in the politico-economic field. Military force is a factor more likely to be effective in maintaining the status quo than in changing it, a factor that has been strengthened by the movement of the political orientation of security policy towards 'defence' rather than 'offence'. However, as force at the higher level becomes less usable as an instrument of change, it appears that the use of low-level violence in the form of international terrorism and armed insurrection by national minorities is becoming more prevalent as a means of political coercion.

If the contention that the future utility of military power is moving towards the maintenance of the status quo, rather than as an effective means of changing it, this has profound implications for the role, shape, and size of the armed forces. There needs to be a rebalancing of some basic priorities of defence policy, such as that between defence against external aggression and the maintenance of internal law and order – an area in which the availability of sophisticated weapons to the terrorist has blurred the boundary that once existed between the civil forces of law and order and the armed services. There is renewed emphasis on the flexi-bility and mobility of armed forces, which carries with it wide implications for their equipment. In the revolutions in eastern Europe, it was the 'look-alike' tank, the helicopter and the armed soldier that played the greatest role. Heavy artillery, long-range rockets, supersonic fighters and sophisticated bombers played no part in the real change of political power.

GLOBAL SECURITY

Whilst NATO has been one of the most successful regional alliances of all time, the global balance of power has for many years been kept between the two superpowers, the United States and the Soviet Union. There is now only one superpower, a situation which leaves no room for a global balance of power. The United States is now effectively the sole agent of the international community in the military enforcement of global security – the 'guarantor of last resort' of international politics – as was demonstrated in the Gulf War. Whilst the United States continues to exercise responsible global leadership, it is not at all clear that the American people will wish to be the 'world's policeman' for all time. The costs are high and there are pressing problems at home. Nor would such a hegemonic role be welcomed in a number of other parts of the world.

The alternative is to aim to build anew a multilateral system of regional and global security and enforcement, which includes a central authority responsible for all aspects of disaster relief, based on the United Nations, in which burdens, risks and responsibilities would be fairly shared throughout the international community. Whilst some would see this as no more than a romantic pipedream, there have been encouraging signs that the UN Security Council may now be able and willing to shoulder the very wide responsibilities that were placed upon it in the Charter, and to exercise the considerable power that nations can provide to it. At the present time, both the European Community in relation to Yugoslavia, and the USA with regard to Iraqi non-compliance with the Gulf War peace terms, are turning to the United Nations for international support and endorsement.

Such a system must provide a balance between global and regional structures. The emergence of a new, wider Europe and the evident need for a new structure for the longer-term peace and security of the Middle East, raise important questions about the development of other regional structures. There has been a proposal for the establishment of a Conference for Security and co-operation in the Mediterranean (CSCM). This proposal may have a part to play in any newly-emerging Middle East order. In the Far East, there have been proposals for some similar form of security structure as a framework for Asian security co-operation – a CSCP (Pacific) perhaps. In Latin America, we see the growing spirit of democracy, and the prospect of greater political and economic stability, leading to the solution of disputes by political rather than military means. The relationship between such regional developments and the United Nations will require very careful consideration. If the United Nations is to act as an effective, overarching global structure to a series of regional security arrangements, then the role of the Security Council, its membership, its mode of operation and its relationship with the still growing General Assembly will need to be re-examined.

THE SECURITY OF EUROPE

Last year's summit of the Conference on Security and Co-operation in Europe (CSCE) reinforced the role of the CSCE by setting up a small, permanent secretariat; by regularizing the processes of political consultation; by setting up a Conflict Prevention Centre; by instituting a parliamentary assembly; and by supporting an office to encourage free and fair elections throughout Europe. Most Western leaders made it clear, however, that, while the CSCE had an important part to play in European security, it had little part to play in European defence. The CSCE could not be regarded as a replacement for NATO, primarily because it commands no means of enforcement. This tacitly recognized the growing need to define more clearly the use of the words 'defence' and 'security'. Whilst there is no agreed rigorous definition of these terms, there is a general understanding that security policy is about political ends and that defence policy is about military means. Security involves the process of political dialogue. Defence involves the structure and operation of armed forces. Security includes risks and challenges that lie outside the field of military competence. Defence ultimately rests on the ability of armed forces to prevail in war.

The prospect of a continuing period of uncertainty about the definition of the future 'Europe' and its political and economic structure may suggest a strong *raison d'être* for the continuation of NATO, broadly as we have known it, as a bastion around which European security may be maintained. There must, however, be doubt whether the continuation of the appearance of the existing security structure is sustainable, at a time when the very basis of the threat to that security has fundamentally changed as a result of the collapse of Communism and the break-up of the Soviet Union. It runs the considerable risk that NATO will lose public support and increasingly be seen to resemble the dinosaur, whose fate we all know.

Of course, NATO is already changing a great deal. It has extended the hand of friendship to its former foes, with whom it is now establishing good military-to-military relations. Ambassadors from former Warsaw Pact countries are 'accredited' to the NATO Head-quarters. NATO has reorganized its ground-force structure, with emphasis being placed on the formation of a new multinational, rapid deployment force. Member states have already announced major reductions in the forces that will be available for NATO assignment. The Alliance has conducted a review of its underlying strategy. It is having to cope with the problems of implementing the Conventional Forces in Europe Treaty. A review of the NATO command structure is underway. NATO is indeed trying hard to come to terms with the problems of defence planning when there is no readily identifiable enemy. Nevertheless, there is a strong suspicion that there is still a great deal in NATO that is not changing. This reflects the view that NATO must continue to stand as a pillar of stability in a sea of uncertainty. NATO has also become such an enormously large and complex organization that even if its disbandment were to be ordered tomorrow, it would still take a long time to run down.

One most important thing that has not changed is NATO's membership, although several former Warsaw Pact countries have declared their wish to join. It is argued that to admit new members at this time would so change the character of NATO that it would no longer be recognizable as an Atlantic Alliance. Furthermore, a major impediment to widening the membership is the strength of the security guarantee provided by Article 5 of the North Atlantic Treaty, that states that an attack on one will be considered as an attack on all.

The continuation of the need for a strong transatlantic security dialogue, for which NATO has over the last 40 years been the principle forum, is predicated on assumptions about the place of the United States in Europe and of the indivisibility of the security of North America and that of western Europe. This has been the basis of the term 'Atlantic security', which carried with it a powerful maritime message that the north Atlantic Ocean was a central feature of that security. Because NATO's use of it for the reinforcement and resupply of Europe was threatened by very powerful Soviet submarine forces, defence of the Atlantic sea lines of communication was a vital interest of the Alliance. Whilst the Soviet/Russian submarine force still exists, it is difficult to foresee circumstances in which it could convincingly pose a threat either to the United States or to western Europe. The very concept of 'Atlantic' security has become blurred. It becomes synonymous with 'European' security. And unless the peoples of both western Europe and the United States are clear as to the interests of both sides that are served by the continuation of the United States as a 'European' power, and as a power in Europe, then no amount of mouthing of the sacred words that American participation in the defence and security of Europe is vital both to Americans and to Europeans will be enough to maintain public support for it, on either side of the Atlantic.

It has been argued that the strategic case for the continuing American involvement in European security rested on the need for the USA to act as a political and military counterbalance to the eastward pull of the mass of Russia and the other members of the Commonwealth of Independent States (CIS) on the countries of central Europe. There was, I believe, much strength in this argument. However, since the failure of the Soviet coup, it is clear that this mass has largely disintegrated, militarily and politically. Even the credibility of the threat posed by Soviet nuclear power is declining as the number of fingers on the former Soviet nuclear safety catch has increased. Thus the need for the presence of American forces on the ground in Europe, either to provide an immediate counter to a conventional attack on NATO territory, or as 'nuclear hostages' giving credibility to American nuclear guarantees, is hardly likely to be enough to convince large elements of Congressional opinion that 'our boys' cannot be brought home. Nonetheless, the American military deployments in peacetime in Europe are seen as an earnest of the wider American interest in the stability of Europe and constitute an important prejudgement of the strategic decision about direct US involvement on the European continent, if that stability were threatened.

Europe needs to recognize that a weakening of the security link between the USA and Europe would almost inevitably accentuate the westward pull of the Asian Pacific region on the United States. Although the emotional ties of most Americans, even on the West Coast, still tend to lie with Europe, and despite increasingly difficult relations with Japan, American trade flows increasingly towards Asian markets. This trend may well be accelerated by the changing ethnic balance of Asians and Hispanics within the United States.

In the 1990 London Declaration, NATO extended the hand of friendship to the East and began the process of strengthening its relationships with the countries of the former Warsaw Pact. At the Council meeting at Copenhagen in June 1991, the member governments, in approving a special statement on partnership with the countries of central and eastern Europe, announced that 'our own security is inseparably linked to that of all other states in Europe'. Whilst this statement was intended to reassure the former Warsaw Pact countries and to prevent a security vacuum from forming on NATO's eastern borders, it fell somewhat short of their aspirations. Since June, a great deal has happened as the Soviet Union has continued to fall apart. If the process of NATO's strengthening of its relations with central and eastern Europe is to continue successfully, as it must, then this will inevitably give rise to growing pressure from these countries for some more formal relationship with the Alliance, including eventual membership. NATO must therefore begin to consider a widening of the Alliance.

DEFENCE AND THE EUROPEAN COMMUNITY

The collapse of Communism in eastern Europe and the Soviet Union, and the emergence of newly-independent states whose declared aim is to become pluralist democracies with market-orientated economies, has added a major new dimension to the problems of the further development of the European Community. At the same time as the two intergovernmental conferences (IGCs) have been addressing the issues of economic/monetary and political union for the existing 12 members, as part of the process of 'deepening' the Community, the list of those countries who are potential applicants for future membership – the process of widening the Community – has grown dramatically. It now numbers more than 20. For many of these potential applicants, the success of their move towards democracy and market economics is heavily dependent on their having market access to western Europe: and particularly for the former Comecon countries, for whom the problems of transition, the need to pay for their energy supplies from the CIS in hard currency, and the almost total collapse of the former Soviet market for their manufactured goods, have had a traumatic effect on their economies. The opening of EC markets to such a potential flow of low-priced goods will inevitably carry significant penalties for Community members. However, if the EC is not willing to respond effectively, then there will be an increasing risk of political instability in eastern Europe and of population migration westwards. Whilst such political instability should not be equated to a military threat to western Europe, there can be no doubt as to its effect on European security, defined in its wider sense. Although it may be possible to envisage an eventual wider European economic area, from 'Brest to Brest', it is extremely difficult to imagine its being paralleled by a political community of such a size along the lines now being negotiated in the two IGCs. In this case where can the elements of defence and security for a wider Europe be fitted in?

Both the British–Italian *Declaration on European Security and Defence* and the Franco–German initiative and draft treaty on political union and common foreign and security policy have recognized the Western European Union (WEU) as the vehicle for developing a common security policy for the union and a stronger European defence identity. There is still disagreement about the position of the WEU with respect to NATO and the EC; but there is now clear agreement that the WEU should be the defence and security arm of the Union.

A NEW NATO

If the membership of the NATO Alliance must eventually be widened, then a revision of the Washington Treaty must be considered. NATO has already been a defensive alliance. It has defended western Europe *against* the Warsaw Pact. There is now no readily identifiable threat *against* which west European countries need now to defend themselves; although there is a growing North/South dimension of European security, enhanced by concern over the possible development of Islamic fundamentalism. The greatest threat to the security of a wider Europe is no longer the threat of external attack, but that of violent, internal division under the pressures of growing nationalism and a potential continuing divide in economic prosperity. This reduces the emphasis that has been placed on the importance of Article 5 of the North Atlantic Treaty that defines an attack upon a member state as being an attack on all. A new 'NATO' treaty would be better based on the fundamental commitment of European states not to initiate armed action against any other member state; and, in the case that such action did occur, to take such action, including military action, as might be necessary to restore the status quo ante and to resolve the issue by peaceful negotiation. Such a treaty would have far greater impact and cohesion than a web of bilateral non-aggression pacts. It would be a revision of the basic NATO treaty. It would be open for signature by all independent European countries that were members of the CSCE. With its signing would come the ending of NATO as we now know it. In this way the 'new NATO' would become the defence arm of the CSCE, in the same way that the WEU can become the defence arm of the European Community.

The new treaty organization would carry forward many of the existing elements of NATO. Like NATO, the new alliance would be both a political and a military alliance. It would have a strong military planning function. In the research, weapon-development and procurement field, it would seek as much rationalization and standardization between national military forces as possible, thus reducing costs and the competitive element in technological development. In the operational planning field, its principle attention would be devoted to peacekeeping contingencies and to disaster relief. It would have a skeleton operational command structure to permit the rapid deployment within Europe of small, highly mobile, multinational units. It would develop common operational procedures and standards, thus permitting the close easy working of national forces, and would conduct joint military exercises. It would have the capability of providing a European contribution to UN operations. It would maintain close relations with the WEU and an Atlantic dimension. It would thus be appropriate to a world moving from bipolar confrontation to multipolar co-operation, from collective defence to collective security.

It has frequently been said that, for the present, the structure of European security, with its many institutions, will inevitably be without any coherent architecture, and that capabilities are more important than structures. But we are in a period of transition – and we do need to have some vision of the eventual position that we would like to reach. It still may be early days in that process of transition. But the violent instability that has already been released does call for vision of a 'new European order'. This has been an attempt to construct the outline of a new security and defence order that is compatible with the trend in the political and economic development of a wider Europe within a new world order.

Reforming NATO's Command and Control Structures

THOMAS-DURELL YOUNG

INTRODUCTION

The ending of the cold war and the blossoming *rapprochement* between NATO and its former adversaries in central and eastern Europe have had a predictable influence on NATO to conform to these new security realities by reforming its strategy and force structure. In consequence, sizeable standing conventional and nuclear forces, arrayed in the Central Region, ever vigilant to meet a short-warning offensive across the now defunct inter-German border, have given way to the Alliance's 'New Strategic Concept', which stresses crisis management, minimal nuclear deterrence and a greater stress on multinational formations.[1] At the same time, it is becoming increasingly evident that the Alliance will be forced to accomplish these new daunting challenges with significant reductions in its members' defence budgets. Indeed, this important consideration alone makes a review of the Alliance's existing military structures essential. To refuse to do so would court the disastrous possibility that the Alliance might lose its political acceptance by its members owing to its military irrelevance to the emerging political and security environment in Europe. And, as vividly demonstrated by persistent European Community (EC) and Western European Union (WEU) efforts to establish a European defence identity (e.g., the Maastricht Summit),[2] there *are* institutional alternatives to NATO, irrespective of their many widely-acknowledged limitations.

Accompanying the 1990–91 review of the Alliance's force structure and strategy has been the less observable move to reassess its future command and control (C^2) requirements for the execution of the new strategic concept.[3] In the final analysis, the redistribution of senior command positions will no doubt prove to be a more politically sensitive task than the reaching of consensus on new Alliance strategic guidance.[4] Since national influence at the highest military levels of the Alliance is at stake in this review process, one can rest assured that the 'primacy of politics' will prevail in the reorganization of these C^2 billets. For instance, all one needs to do is to review the press reports of the acrimonious debate which took place in public during the first half of 1991 between Britain and the Federal Republic of Germany over which country would lead the Alliance's new Allied Command Europe (ACE) Rapid Reaction Corps[5] in order to appreciate the political sensitivity that surrounds this issue.

Some preliminary decisions to rationalize and reorganize existing C^2 structures were announced at the Defence Planning Committee (DPC) meeting in December 1991,[6] albeit a more comprehensive explanation of C^2 restructuring has yet to be presented in public. In general, the overarching C^2 structure of the integrated military command has been announced, while subordinate levels of command are in the process of being reorganized. At the highest level, the United States will retain leadership of its two major NATO commands (MNCs), Supreme Allied Commander Atlantic and Supreme Allied Commander Europe (SACEUR). Britain has lost its previous MNC, Allied Commander-in-Chief, Channel (CINCHAN).[7] While apparently not completed, there are some indications as to how the major subordinate commands (MSCs) and principal subordinate commands (PSCs) in ACE will be reorganized, in addition to some indications as to how C^2 will be exercised over the rapid reaction formations, which are currently being organized. Moreover, it is possible to identify from public sources current and future points of contention in the Alliance which will make C^2 reorganization difficult. These areas of contention include residual disagreements over the proposed C^2 structures for Allied Forces Northern Europe (AFNORTH), the rapid reaction formations and the perennial problems associated with Allied Forces Southern Europe (AFSOUTH). Furthermore, AFCENT will also undergo many changes as it reorganizes and rationalizes its C^2 structures owing, in part, to the efforts by Germany to 'normalize' selective aspects of its defence structures.

This article will argue that the political ramifications emanating from the ending of the cold war necessitate a revamping of the Alliance C^2 organization. Whether one likes it or not, the process of national disintegration (as one currently sees it in the former Soviet Union and Yugoslavia) and the alteration of borders (as produced by the unification of Germany) cannot necessarily be controlled to the benefit of the West in all cases. Current supranational political and security structures in Europe are being shown to be ill-suited to deal with new forms of actual and potential conflict in and adjacent to the European phoenix emerging from the ashes of the cold war. If NATO's supporters wish it to be capable of responding to these new crises in, not to mention outside, Europe, and thereby maintain a position whereby to exert a positive force to resolve conflicts, then the means to exercise C^2 over Alliance military forces must change.

CONTEMPORARY PROBLEMS FACING MSCs IN ACE

The rapid transformation of the European security landscape, from one that was dominated by East–West bloc confrontation to one which is today slowly evolving toward a threat-ambiguous, albeit not barren, environment, has presented NATO with new challenges, while bringing to the surface longstanding, unresolved problems in NATO's C^2 arrangements. This section will briefly describe some of the more difficult issues which will need to be addressed in ACE as the Alliance reforms its C^2 structures for the immediate term. It needs to be mentioned at the outset that political and even military rationales would seem to dictate that the current alignment of three geographically-defined MSCs under ACE (north, central and south) be maintained. The reason for this is that the geographic singularity of each region is such as to require one headquarters to concentrate its efforts toward planning and conducting campaigns in each region. This does not imply that intra-MSC transfer of forces during a crisis should not be encouraged; and indeed, the future course of the Alliance could well dictate this. Rather, the requirements of C^2 at the theatre level are such as to necessitate the maintenance of at least three MSCs, or MSC-like commands in ACE. Note that two current MSCs in ACE, UK Air Forces Command (UK AIR) and the ACE Mobile Force (AMF), Land and Air, will not be dealt with separately, since they themselves, or their responsibilities, will apparently be subsumed by the new Allied Forces Northwestern Europe Command (AFNORTHWEST) and rapid reaction forces, respectively.

Allied Forces Central Europe (AFCENT)

The AFCENT region stands to change fundamentally during the next few years because much of the positive change in the previous external security environment directly impacts upon it. Under current arrangements,[8] five PSCs report to the AFCENT commander (a German four-star general). The ground component consists of the Northern Army Group (NORTHAG) and Central Army Group (CENTAG). A British four-star general commands NORTHAG and also the British Army of the Rhine, while CENTAG is commanded by a US four-star general who is also US Army Commander, Europe. As regards air power, Allied Air Forces Central Europe (a US Air Force four-star general) exercises C^2 over 2nd Allied Tactical Air Forces (commanded by a British three-star general) and 4th Allied Tactical Air Force (commanded by a German three-star general).

The central problem associated with this structure is that, in a numerical sense, forward-deployed and standing ground and air units will diminish significantly in short order. Shrinking national defence budgets, the implementation of the CFE Treaty and the withdrawal of the Soviet Western Group of Forces from eastern Germany will all contribute to this end. This, in turn, has resulted in placing political pressure on NATO to rationalize its C^2 structure to conform with a diminished force structure. In an operational sense as well, the unification of Germany has presented the Alliance with a significant change in AFCENT's future area of operation, albeit this is currently complicated by the provisions of the 'Two-Plus-Four' Treaty. In consequence, there are strong rationales for AFCENT's PSCs to be restructured, which would bring its C^2 headquarters into line with new Alliance force-structure guidelines; these envisage the designation of forces as main defence, rapid reaction and augmentation. At the Defense Planning Committee meeting in December 1991 it was agreed that AFCENT should amalgamate its current five PSC headquarters into two.[9]

Specific to the Army Groups, two broad issues will have to be faced in the near future. The first relates to the simple numbers of allied forces in the area of responsibility of AFCENT (in addition to problems associated with the exercising of C^2 over multinational units). It can be expected that the two allied Army Group commands (PSCs) in the AFCENT region will be combined into one (LANDCENT),[10] in view of the decreasing number of army corps assigned/earmarked for the region. Currently, eight allied army corps are assigned to the AFCENT region, which are scheduled to fall to seven (albeit with one German Corps stationed in eastern Germany), in addition to the yet to be organized ACE Rapid Reaction Corps.[11] Of course, the span of control over subordinate units is generally accepted as ranging from three to five sub-units. However, the reorganization of main defence forces, to employ the new NATO nomenclature, into multinational corps, not to mention the creation of the ACE Rapid Reaction Corps, has reduced the size of the main defence and projected augmentation forces to make the current two Army Groups structure redundant.

Immediately below the Army Groups, the organization of remaining corps into multinational formations will need to be carried out in the near future. For the short term, the establishment of C^2 over the proposed multinational corps structure will not be too difficult to achieve since true integration has been rejected. The model for the exercise of C^2 over most, if not all, of these formations would appear to be that of the US Army VII Corps–12th *Panzer* Division relationship where 'integration' is limited to the transfer of operational control of units at the division level.[12] Over the longer term, however, problems could develop as European nations alter force structure and doctrine in an era of limited manpower and finances. For instance, the US Army is currently structured whereby the corps is the principal level of C^2 to prosecute operational missions in a theatre.[13] Consequently, the corps commander has a considerable range of assets at his disposal for temporary allocation to lower commanders for the specific missions he has directed to be accomplished. In the German Army, on the other hand, it is the divisional commander who has this responsibility, as well as the military assets, thus, the large size of German divisions (21,250 for *Panzer* divisions; 21,500 for *Panzergrenadier* divisions).[14] There is, however, currently discussion in German defence circles that, as a result of the numerical limitation of 370,000 placed on the *Bundeswehr* as a result of the Two Plus Four Treaty, a more efficient usage of limited personnel could eventually result in greater C^2 authority and more assets for brigade commanders.[15]

Therefore if multinationality of ground forces is to become effective in an operational sense, difficult challenges could present themselves to participating national armies when greater integration is pressed. In this respect, the current doctrinal debate in the US Army to press for the adoption of similar structures (i.e., to concentrate greater C^2 authority and assets at the brigade level) takes on greater importance.[16] To make US Army brigades more combat independent could also take on political importance if the United States decides to participate in proposals to cross-station European and North American forces throughout Europe as a means of offsetting the 'singularization' of any one country.[17] While admittedly a stationing, short of a war-fighting deployment, the fielding of independent brigades would convey a war-fighting character which could underscore Washington's continued commitment to western European security and stability.

One final aspect of multinationality needs to be discussed. This concerns efforts to establish a defence element of the EC, the most recent effort being the October 1991 proposal by Chancellor Kohl and President Mitterrand to create a European Corps, based upon the current Franco-German brigade,[18] which, following the Maastricht Summit, would fall under the WEU.[19] While there is considerable confusion over what might eventually develop from such proposals, and others that will surely follow, the creation of such a formation need not necessarily result in C^2 difficulties with NATO structures.[20] In explaining the European Corps proposal, Chancellor Kohl was adamant that any German contribution of force to this proposed formation would be done only on the basis of 'dual-hatting'.[21] This is to say, that German contributions would keep their NATO designated missions, but would also assume other missions under whatever type of C^2 structure the WEU may ultimately develop. As other European countries reduce their own defence structures, it can be expected that the Alliance could well see a greater degree of dual-hatting by European states, should a solely European formation be created. What needs to be defined at the outset of the creation of such a formation is a clear division of efforts and responsibilities between it (e.g., out-of-area) and NATO C^2 authorities (e.g., in-area), so as to avoid any perceived or actual conflicting responsibilities.[22]

As regards Allied Tactical Air Forces in the Central Region, the *Luftwaffe* now has the responsibility for the policy of German airspace, a role previously exercised largely by the United States and Britain. Moreover, since unification the *Luftwaffe* has sole responsibility for the air defence over the former territory of the German Democratic Republic.[23] Under the terms of the Two Plus Four Treaty, these *Luftwaffe* assets must operate outside NATO air defence structures until the end of 1994. After that date, NATO and the Federal Republic must decide what should replace the present air defence arrangements in the east.[24] These new operating conditions will surely necessitate a review of existing air defence C^2 arrangements in the Central Region, albeit with added provisions for rapid expansion in time of crises. Under current plans, 2nd and 4th Allied Tactical Air Force headquarters will be combined to form AIRCENT headquarters.[25]

Secondly, both air and ground C^2 structures in AFCENT will be strongly influenced by a little appreciated move by the Federal Republic to 'normalize' selectively parts of its defence capabilities. Since the arming of the Federal Republic in 1955, the *Bundeswehr* has lacked key capabilities and structures, which has made the national employment of military force of any size in a joint setting almost an impossibility.[26] It needs to be stressed that too much should not be read into this initiative. The creation of a balanced national defence capability by the Federal Republic does not imply the *ipso facto* re-emergence of an atavistic and nationalist external policy by Bonn, let alone the 'nationalization' of Germany's defences.[27]

The implications of this logical outcome of the unification of, and restoration of full sovereignty to, Germany will affect the manner by which allied C^2 structures in the AFCENT region will operate, because of these new national German C^2 structures. As regards the need for the Federal Republic to develop its own national C^2 structures, following the unification of the two Germanies on 3 October 1990 Bonn assumed responsibility for the defence of the territory of the former German Democratic Republic. In view of the fact that the Bonn government has gone on record as stating that there will be no 'special security zones' in a unified Germany,[28] a national capability to conduct operations unilaterally is unquestionably required.

The consequence of this new responsibility to defend its five new, eastern

Länder is the move by Bonn to create a new national C^2 structure. As already mentioned above, the *Luftwaffe* has the new mission of providing for the policing of air space over western and eastern Germany.[29] The *Bundesmarine* will be the service least affected, in view of the fact that it already has substantial service C^2 structures, although it is scheduled to face sizeable reductions of personnel and vessel numbers, and is to move its Navy Office east to Rostock.[30] The German Army will be the most affected by the new C^2 arrangements. Considerable attention has been directed to the merging of the field and the territorial army into joint headquarters in order to save personnel (initially put at 10,000 military and 1,600 civilian positions), which in itself blurs the distinction which formerly existed between NATO-designated and national-commanded territorial formations.[31] Moreover, the former III *Korps* headquarters located in Koblenz has been moved to Potsdam where it has assumed responsibility for the ground defence of the eastern *Länder*. To be sure, *Bundeswehr* units in eastern Germany may be fully integrated into NATO C^2 structures after 1994, thereby obviating the need for new and expensive national C^2 capabilities. It would appear, however, that Bonn has chosen to eschew this form of self-singularization and *limited* national C^2 capabilities are being created.[32]

Surprisingly lost to many have been the C^2 implications of these actions. The move to create at Koblenz the new *Heeresführungs-kommando* (Army Command Headquarters) provides the means to exercise C^2 over the army.[33] Once established, the Federal Republic will have the ability to conduct independent army operations above corps level for the first time. Since the arming of the Federal Republic in 1955, C^2 above corps level has been provided by the AFCENT commander. Moreover, to provide C^2 in a joint sense over all three services, *Streitkräfte führungskommando* (Joint Armed Forces Command) will be created, also to be located in Koblenz. Once this structure is created, it would provide the *Bundeswehr* for the first time with joint operational control capability. This normalization of the Federal Republic's defences will include, in time, the eventual formulation of national war plans (to complement NATO planning), an element of national defence which has heretofore been provided by NATO.[34]

What the development of a national C^2 structure on the part of the *Bundeswehr* means is that future allied C^2 arrangements in the Federal Republic must accommodate future German C^2 organization command billets. As it now stands, a number of questions should be addressed. For instance, what will be the future C^2 responsibilities of AFCENT (a German four-star general) at a time when there could be a German commander exercising C^2 over all *Bundeswehr* forces in unified Germany? How comfortable would Europe feel if a German four-star general were nominated to be dual-hatted in both roles? And what type of C^2 relationship should exist between the *Bundeswehr* commands in Koblenz and the remaining allied forces in the Federal Republic? These are only some of the questions which will have to be addressed over the mid-term. However, what is important to understand is that, just as conditions have changed fundamentally in the former Warsaw Pact countries, so has the political and military basis by which AFCENT will function in the Federal Republic as it slowly normalizes elements of its defence capabilities.

Allied Forces North (AFNORTH)

Considerable controversy has been generated by the review of future C^2 requirements in the Nordic region. The problem is essentially related to the longstanding issue of Norway's insistence upon having a link to the Central Region through NATO C^2 structures and Germany's desire to unify its territory under one MSC. In attempting to assuage national sensitivities and realign C^2 structures to the altered security realities of the Nordic region, the proposed arrangement appears to be complicated at best and possibly unworkable at worst, according to Norwegian officials.

In essence, Norway has long been fearful that its allies to the south in the Central Region might ignore its security concerns in a crisis.[35] While the security situation in central Europe may have changed for the better following the dissolution of the Warsaw Pact and the disintegration of the Soviet Union, this improvement has not been mirrored in northern Norway from the point of view of Oslo. For example, the transfer of Soviet military equipment from the Central Region to the Kola peninsula during 1990 and 1991 resulted in a public threat in May 1991 made by the Norwegian Defence Minister, Johan Holst, that Norway would not ratify the CFE Treaty unless Oslo's concerns over this build-up in conventional forces were met.[36] The Norwegian press has reported that government officials have been strongly opposed to any initiative in NATO that would result in AFNORTH's area of responsibility being cut off from the Central Region.[37] The longstanding inclusion of northern Germany in AFNORTH has been seen as being of fundamental importance to Norwegian security, since Oslo is neither a member of the EC nor the WEU.

Under current arrangements, the LANDJUT multinational corps, comprising 6th German *Panzergrenadier* Division and the Danish Mechanized Jutland Division, fall under the C^2 of Commander Allied Forces Baltic Approach, a PSC of AFNORTH. The Federal Republic has insisted that it will no longer be the sole NATO member whose territory falls under two MSCs, and that the border between the two commands must be shifted northward of the German border.[38] By effecting this change, Bonn would then be able to concentrate the German Army, which must shrink from 48 to 28 manoeuvre brigades by 1994, into eastern Germany in a crisis, as opposed to its being tied to what has become, for all intents and purposes, a rearward area (i.e., Schleswig-Holstein). Bonn's responsibility to defend the coastal area of the former German Democratic Republic also lends strong support to the redesignation of the responsibility and forces of this area to AFCENT. Consequently, the LANDJUT Corps and the AFNORTH/AFCENT border, as configured in the past to meet an offensive by the Warsaw Pact, are no longer relevant.

As a result of much acrimonious debate in the Alliance, a proposed solution to meet both Germany's and Norway's interests has reportedly been adopted. According to Defence Minister Holst,[39] Schleswig-Holstein and Denmark would become part of AFCENT. NATO's Northern Command at Kolsas will be dissolved in its current configuration. CINCHAN, it will be recalled, is to be dissolved, but in its place AFNORTHWEST is to be set up based at Northwood in Britain, headed by a British commander. This headquarters will assume responsibility for the air and land defence of the British Isles and Norway, in addition to the sea defence of the English Channel, the North Sea, and the Baltic Sea. In consequence, AFNORTHWEST would exercise control over Belgian, Dutch, Norwegian, Danish, and German naval units. As a result of the creation of this new headquarters, BALTAP in Denmark and a new as yet unnamed allied headquarters in Norway (headed by a Norwegian) will also report to AFNORTHWEST.[40]

One could see where this proposed structure will anger many and please few. It makes little basic operational sense that the air and land defence of Denmark and the German Baltic coast are an AFCENT responsibility, while Northwestern Command (in the United Kingdom) is responsible for the Baltic Sea. While Germany succeeded in removing the singularlization of having its territory divided between two MSCs, it did have to give the *Bundesmarine* to AFNORTHWEST. The Norwegians have lost their *pied-à-terre* in the Central Region, despite the creation of AFNORTHWEST and the establishment of a new NATO headquarters in Norway to be headed by a Norwegian, as opposed to a British general under the existing AFNORTH C^2 structure. Even Britain has reason to be dissatisfied. Albeit gaining leadership over AFNORTHWEST, it would lose its of AFNORTH command, in addition, presumably, to the previous UK AIR command. Additionally, under this proposal, the United Kingdom, for the first time, would become part of ACE.

Even if one were to assume that this new arrangement would function well in peacetime and even in crisis or war (and this could be seen as being problematic), the fact remains that, at a time when the Alliance is attempting to reassure *all* of its members of the continued relevance of NATO, Norway perceives that it is being marginalized. As argued in an editorial in *Aftenposten*, NATO runs the risk of conveying to the Norwegian public that it no longer finds Norway so interesting. However, as recognised in the same editorial, Norway itself must put its own house in order.[41] One would assume that this refers to the fact that Norwegian anxieties of being isolated from their allies in central Europe could be mitigated through Oslo's own efforts to join the WEU, whose treaty provisions (Article IV of the modified Brussels Treaty) for mutual security support and assistance are *stronger* than those of NATO.[42] Notwithstanding this fact, it would seem that the C^2 controversy in the AFNORTH/AFNORTHWEST area will continue to plague NATO for some time.

Allied Forces South (AFSOUTH)

Over the years, AFSOUTH has been a relative backwater in European security. This has been due to the mission of this headquarters, which has essentially been one of securing the Mediterranean and serving as a conduit to move air and ground reinforcement forces to the eastern Mediterranean in an emergency. However, in view of the many uncertainties present in this region, it could be expected that the southern NATO partners will wish to maintain at a minimum, if not to expand, existing C^2 arrangements to conform to the emergence of new risks to collective security.[43] A survey of the individual security situations of key southern allies is sobering.[44]

Ankara continues to see large military forces stationed and emerging across its vulnerable eastern borders in the former Soviet Republics which have gained independence and have traditionally had strong antipathies toward each other, not to mention toward Turkey. Added to this is the presence of such potentially destabilizing states as Iraq and Syria on Ankara's eastern and southern border. For its part, Rome has expressed concern that the improved security situation in central Europe could result in Italy's becoming decoupled from its close allies to the north at a time when the Maghreb shows signs of becoming destabilized through the rise in popularity of Islamic fundamentalist movements. In France, home to over four million Muslims, domestic political conflicts with Muslim immigrants have been exacerbated by fear that a radical north African state might attempt to support the claims of their 'oppressed' brethren in Europe through the use of long-range weapons of mass destruction.[45] According to one press report, this anxiety on the part of the southern Alliance members has not been ignored by NATO and is being addressed in its current planning.[46]

In view of the fact that the centre of gravity in terms of threat/risk perceptions could well be shifting southward,[47] the Alliance may wish to rethink its current C^2 arrangements for the entire region. After all, there are elements of the current structure which are incomplete. For instance, even though Greece returned to the Integrated Military Command system on 20 October 1980, it does not participate in all of the C^2 arrangements of the Alliance in the region. Consequently, the task of achieving C^2 co-ordination by the Alliance has been challenging at best.[48]

One proposal to overcome intra-alliance political sensitivities over inter-allied co-operation between NATO partners is to create allied C^2 arrangements, where appropriate, along functional lines with omnidirectional orientation where possible.[49] For instance, while generally only thought of as a Central Region state, France is also a Mediterranean power with strong security interests in that region. Perhaps France's long standing opposition to participating in NATO C^2 structures could be mitigated should functional C^2 arrangements be employed which were addressed to the contingencies Paris finds of immediate importance.[50] In view of Rome's central location in the Mediterranean and past strong political commitment to the Alliance, Italy would be a logical choice for the basing of some headquarters to exercise C^2 over these functional formations.[51] Thus should a multinational corps/division with Italian, Portuguese, Greek and Turkish forces be organized, as has been proposed, Italy would be the logical location for its headquarters and associated standing support elements.[52]

Rapid Reaction Forces

Rapid reaction capabilities in ACE are currently limited to AMF Land and Air, which will be greatly augmented in the near future through the creation of the ACE Rapid Reaction Corps. The commander of the AMF Land is a two-star general, whose nationality is rotated among the contributing members. As an MSC it is directly under the C^2 of SACEUR. The AMF is planned to increase in size and become the 'Immediate Reaction' element of the ACE Rapid Reaction Corps. A complication in its status is sure to arise out of the need for the Alliance to define its new C^2 relationship with the ACE Rapid Reaction Corps, which the Defence Policy Committee agreed to establish at its May 1991 meeting.[53]

At this point, the only C^2 issue apparently resolved concerning the ACE Rapid Reaction Corps is that it will be commanded by a British officer (three-star general) and a multinational Reaction Force Planning Staff will be established at SHAPE. This planning staff is to develop and co-ordinate plans for all ACE Reaction Forces.[54] Left unresolved are the important questions of whether the force will be a PSC, and if so, under which MSC, or if it will be an MSC in its own right. A complication has already arisen in regard to German demands that the air component of the Rapid Reaction Corps should be headed by a *Luftwaffe* three-star general.[55] Just how such a C^2 arrangement would work remains to be seen. What is clear is that German anger over the decision in spring 1991 giving Britain leadership of the Corps shows no sign of abating.[56]

Also left undefined is how the naval elements of the rapid reaction force are to be commanded. According to Dutch official sources, two task groups will comprise the Naval Reaction Forces and will be deployed to the Atlantic and the Mediterranean. The core of these two standing groups will be designated as Immediate Reaction Forces. These task forces will be derived from existing Standing Naval Force Atlantic and Naval On-Call Force Mediterranean.[57]

A potential problem may arise should some European officials, wishing to accentuate the European character of the rapid reaction forces, oppose the placing of them under the direct C^2 of SACEUR, who is, of course, an American four-star general and is likely to remain so. However, in view of the fact that the ACE Rapid Reaction Corps will consist of some undetermined US air and logistic support assets[58] and indeed, that these contributions will be essential if the force is to have any force projection capabilities,[59] it would be ludicrous for the formation not to come under SACEUR. Indeed, one could expect that the deterrence value of the Rapid Reaction Corps would be greatly enhanced by significant US participation and direct linkage to SACEUR.

Additionally, the relationship between the Alliance's rapid reaction and main defence forces needs to be considered at this early stage. In view of the planned lower levels of readiness of main defence forces in the future, it is not inconceivable that rapid reaction forces will deploy to a region before its main defence forces are fully mobilized. To ensure clarity of C^2 responsibilities, it would make sense to have rapid reaction formations effect the transfer of authority of C^2 from SACEUR to the MSC in the area to which they are deployed once they are combat ready.

Finally, the ability of a commander to exercise C^2 over his assigned units is highly dependent upon the communication systems available to him. As it is given that there will be fewer conventional standing and reserve forces in NATO in the future, the need for modern command, control, communications, and intelligence (C^3I) capabilities will be a *sine qua non*, particularly for reaction formations. These capabilities are not inexpensive and it is problematic whether many Alliance countries in an era of defence penury will be able to obtain these sophisticated and expensive capabilities. Consideration, therefore, should be given to the procurement by NATO of mobile variants of these C^3I systems. It would not be necessary to have a complete set for each and every possible envisaged headquarters, but rather enough to support a certain number of contingencies, as determined by the Alliance leadership. The possibility of the procurement of these systems would be enhanced at the political level if it were argued that they would support the Alliance's stated goal of engaging in effective crisis management, since they could support operations ranging from civil peace-monitoring to military intervention.

It is imperative that these outstanding issues related to the C^2 of the Alliance's rapid reaction forces be resolved successfully, since the ultimate political fate of NATO could depend, in part, upon how successful these formations appear. The evolution of the European security environment makes it apparent that the future relevance of NATO will be strongly influenced by how well it develops its capability to engage in effective crisis management. In support of this Alliance objective, its rapid reaction formations will play a key role. When one considers possible contingencies in which these forces could be committed (i.e., central Europe, the Balkans, Norway and eastern Turkey), it is apparent that the extreme sensitivity in the mere deployment of forces, let alone their actual employment, will be crucial.

CONCLUSION

That NATO's C^2 structures are changing fundamentally is without question. As European security conditions continue their rapid transformation toward an uncertain future, it is only logical that these structures should be altered accordingly. The difficult challenge to the leaders of the Western alliance is in reforming existing C^2 arrangements to meet immediate security conditions in Europe while laying the necessary foundations for future structures which are likely to be needed by mid-decade.

The need for flexible C^2 structures, readily applicable to a wide range of crisis scenarios and variable force configurations, could be seen as presenting the Alliance with its most immediate requirements in the post-cold war period. Indeed, one may already observe how trends in European security conditions are developing. Examples of national disintegration in Europe have occurred (i.e., the former-Soviet Union), which in turn have established a number of unpleasant post-cold war precedents. The civil war in Yugoslavia is the first European war since 1945. The unification of Germany on 3 October 1990 constituted the first significant change in European borders since the end of the Second World

War. In a region with long historical memories and innumerable irredentist claims based on history and the presence of ethnic minorities, the occurrence of these development points to a much different security environment than was the case in the cold war: one that is fraught with risks for the western Alliance.

The implications for NATO of these changes in European security are no doubt immense and need to be reflected in the Alliance's C^2 arrangements to respond to threats and risks to common security. In this respect it would appear that, while the proposed transformation of NATO's C^2 structure is significant, events could demonstrate that the reform process has actually only just begun. The reason for this assertion is that, in view of the difficulty which has apparently surrounded the restructuring of AFNORTH, one can only imagine the 'challenge' that will face the Alliance when it tries its hand at reforming AFSOUTH, particularly if Spain and France are to be brought into their command arrangement. While not wishing to appear to be determinist, the immense geographic size of AFSOUTH's responsibilities and its many disparate sub-regions and intra-alliance political conflicts could make the reforming of it in a strictly geographical sense, as mentioned above, almost a herculean task.

What the Alliance may wish to contemplate, therefore, is to progressively establish mobile functional formations (e.g., reaction combat, reaction combat support, reaction combat service support), in place of geographic-designated ones; albeit without obviating the self-defence capabilities of the Alliance's armed forces, or changing the current geographic delineation of the three MSCs. The advantages of this approach would be to give subordinate PSC commanders a greater omni-directional orientation, in place of specific geographic ones, which could obviate political frictions. The Alliance appears to be already beginning to adopt this approach to C^2 as illustrated by the creation of the ACE Rapid Reaction Corps and the proposed multinational corps made up of AFSOUTH allies. The necessary complement to this proposed C^2 structure is logistical and transport capabilities, in which many European allies are very weak. Overcoming this challenge in a time of diminishing defence budgets could well prove to the most difficult challenge the Alliance will have to face over the mid-term.

It is also essential to US security interests in Europe that NATO C^2 structures *remain* visibly relevant to European security requirements, and not merely exist in an institutional sense. Fortunately, Washington's European allies and the newly emerging democracies in central and eastern Europe are strongly in favour of the United States remaining active in European affairs within a healthy NATO. As a country that has never harboured territorial ambitions in Europe, the USA's participation in NATO will arguably give that organization (as distinct from the EC or WEU) legitimacy to resolve and to intervene in some inter-regional conflicts in Europe. And until the Conference on Security and Co-operation in Europe (CSCE) reaches its full maturity, NATO will remain as Washington's key institutional entrée to European security affairs.

From the viewpoint of US interests, there should be a high degree of immediacy attached to the reformation of C^2 structures. The Alliance will have to compete progressively more with proposals to create a European defence identity, which may, over time, include plans which could negatively affect NATO C^2 structures. Consequently, remaining NATO C^2 arrangements will take on increased political importance within the Alliance at a time when there will be fewer other publicly noticeable aspects of it. Since US policy has identified that NATO will remain the key organizational linkage it has to Europe, Washington should press vigorously for the alteration of C^2 structures. For not to do so, or if American efforts end in failure, Washington will lose a key instrument of influence over European affairs and stability.

ACKNOWLEDGEMENTS

The views expressed in this article are those of the author and do not necessarily reflect the official policy or position of the Department of the Army, the Department of Defense, or the US Government. The author would like to express his thanks to Lieutenant Colonel William Johnsen and Colonels John Hickey and William Berry for their constructive comments made on earlier drafts.

NOTES

1. 'The Alliance's New Strategic Concept', Press Communiqué S–1(91)85, Brussels: NATO Press Service, 7 November 1991.
2. *Washington Post*, 12 December 1991.
3. This was initiated at the May 1991 Defense Planning Committee and Nuclear Planning Group meeting: '. . . we have agreed that a study of NATO's command structure should be pursued as a matter of urgency with the aim of streamlining and adapting it to the new situation.' See 'Final Communique', Press Communiqué M–DPC/NPG–1(91)38, Brussels: NATO Press Service, 29 May 1991.
4. Michel Fortmann, 'NATO Defense Planning in a Post–CFE Environment: Assessing the Alliance Strategy Review (1990–1991)', in *Homeward Bound? Allied Forces in the New Germany*, Boulder, CO: Westview Press, 1992, pp. 41–63.
5. *Die Welt*, 27 May 1991; and, 'Britische Dominanz bei NATO–Eingreiftruppe: NATO–Streitkräftestruktur mit Fragezeichen', *IAP-Dienst*, (11), 6 June 1991, pp.4–6.
6. 'Final Communique of the Defense Planning Committee of the North Atlantic Treaty Organization', Press Communiqué M–DPC2(91)104, Brussels: NATO Press Service, 13 December 1991.
7. Ibid.

8. For details on the NATO command structure, see Bruce George (ed.), *Jane's NATO Handbook, 1989–1990*, Coulsdon: Jane's Defence Data, 1989, pp.115–54.
9. Note 6.
10. *European Stars and Stripes*, 4 December 1991.
11. Note 3.
12. Frederick M. Franks and Alan T. Carver, 'Building a NATO Corps', *Military Review*, Vol.71, No.7, July 1991, pp.30–2.
13. *FM 100–5 Operations*, Washington, DC: Department of the Army, May 1986.
14. 'JDW Interview with General Klaus Naumann', *Jane's Defence Weekly*, 5 October 1991, p.636.
15. Ibid. and Dr Dieter Ose, 'Operational Command and Control', Bonn: Ministry of Defence, March 1991, draft m/s.
16. This is expounded in the document, *AIRLAND Operations: the Evolution of AirLand Battle for a Strategic Army*, Final Draft, Ft Monroe, VA: TRADOC, Pam 525–5b, 13 June 1991. Note that this debate is taking place within the context of the rewriting of the *FM 100–5 Operations* document. It is expected that a draft of this new edition may be available by late 1992. For background, see James R. McDonough, 'Building the New FM 100–5: Process and Product', *Military Review*, Vol.71, No.10, October 1991, pp.2–12.
17. For background on this issue, see David S. Yost, 'France and West European Defence Identity', *Survival*, Vol.33, No.4, July-August 1991, pp.328–31.
18. *Financial Times*, 16 October 1991. A text of the security initiatives is found in *Le Monde*, 17 October 1991.
19. *Washington Post*, 12 December 1991.
20. *Independent*, 22 October 1991.
21. *Frankfurter Allgemeine*, 7 November 1991.
22. In any case, the Franco-German 'European Corps' proposal is not without its critics owing to its lack of 'reality'. See Michael Inacker's excellent piece in *Rheinischer Merkur*, 25 October 1991.
23. Geoffrey Van Orden, 'The *Bundeswehr* in Transition', *Survival*, Vol.33, No.4, July-August 1991, p.368.
24. See Treaty on the Final Settlement with Respect to Germany, Moscow, 12 September 1991, Article 5 (1).
25. *European Stars and Stripes*, 4 December 1991.
26. 'The *Bundeswehr* has been conceived as an army in the Alliance and not as an instrument for independent military power projection on the part of the Federal Republic of Germany . . . Therefore, the fighting units of the *Bundeswehr*, with the exception of some units of the Territorial Army, are intended to be placed under the operational control of NATO.' *White Paper 1985: The Situation and Development of the Federal Armed Forces*, Bonn: Federal Minister of Defence, 1985, p.72.
27. Van Orden p.353.
28. Cf. comments by German Defence Minister Stoltenberg and Foreign Minister Genscher in, *DPA* (Hamburg), 15 May 1990 in *FBIS–WEU–90–094, 15 May 1990, pp.18–19; and ADN International Service*, 18 July 1990 in *FBIS–WEU–90–139, 19 July 1990, p.11.
29. Joerg Kuebart, 'No Restructuring Without a Price: Prospects and Parameters of *Luftwaffe* Structure 4', *Europäische Sicherheit*, No.9, September 1991, pp.502–8 in *FBIS–WEU–91–212–A*, 1 November 1991, pp.2–6.
30. Volker Hogrebe, 'Bound for the Future – New Structure for the Navy', *Schiff & Haffen/Seewirschaft* No.6, June 1991, pp.14–18, *FBIS–WEU91 147*, 31 July 1991, pp.17–18.
31. Ulrich Weisser, 'Die Weichen sind gestellt: Rahmenbedingungen und Gruntentscheidungen zur Bundeswehrgesamtplanung', *Soldat und Technik*, Vol.34, No.3, March 1991, pp. 159–62.
32. *Bundeswehr Kommando Ost*, located in Strausberg, was created on 3 October 1990, as an interim measure, to oversee the amalgamation of select elements and personnel of the former *Nationale Volksarmee*. This headquarters was dissolved on 1 July 1991,

when these newly integrated *Bundeswehr* formations in the new *Länder* came under the C² of their respective services, albeit outside NATO, as agreed to in July 1990 by Chancellor Kohl and President Gorbachev in Stavropol and codified in the September 1990 'Two-Plus-Four Treaty'.

33. For an excellent analysis of the restructuring of the German Army and its new command organizations, see Erhard Drew, *et al.*, 'Das neue deutsche Heer: Zielsetzung, Konzeption und Elemente der Heerestruktur 5', *Truppenpraxis*, No.4, 1991, pp.356–67.
34. Information provided by German official sources.
35. *Aftenposten*, 3 September 1991.
36. *Sovetskaya Rossiya*, 29 May 1991, in *FBIS–SOV–91–105*, 31 May 1991, p.2.
37. *Aftenposten*, 16 October 1991, in *FBIS–WEU–91–202*, 18 October 1991, p.32.
38. Ibid., 22 October 1991, in *FBIS–WEU–91–209*, 29 October 1991, p.38.
39. Ibid., 29 November 1991, in *FBIS–WEU–91–242*, 29 December 1991, pp. 40–1.
40. *Defense News*, 9 December 1991.
41. *Aftenposten*, 26 October 1991, in *FBIS–WEU–90–221*, 15 November 1991, p.36.
42. For an assessment on the enlargement issue, see Nicole Gnesotto, 'European Defence: Why not the Twelve?' *Chaillot Papers* No.1, Paris: Institute for Security Studies, Western European Union, March 1991.
43. *Guardian*, 4 November 1991.
44. For an excellent assessment of contemporary security challenges facing Alliance members in AFSOUTH, see Roberto Aliboni, 'European Security Across the Mediterranean', *Chaillot Papers* No.2, Paris: Institute for Security Studies, Western European Union, March 1991.
45. John Newhouse, 'The Diplomatic Round: a Collective Nervous Breakdown', *New Yorker*, 2 September 1991, pp.88–9.
46. *Defense News*, 29 April 1991.
47. See Draft Interim Report by the Subcommittee on the Southern Region, Political Committee, North Atlantic Assembly, PC/SR (91) 5, Brussels: International Secretariat, October 1991.
48. Mark Stenhouse and Bruce George, 'NATO's Southern Region', (note 8), pp.133–4.
49. This argument is made by the current commander of Allied Naval Forces Baltic Approaches, VADM Klaus Rehder, in *Wehrtechnik*, No.11, November 1991, p.32.
50. For background on the current French defence debate regarding the Alliance (see note 17), pp.327–51.
51. Note that Defence Minister Joxe has expressed displeasure with France's being one of the few European countries that does not participate in many NATO meetings. See *The Times*, 4 December 1991.
52. See the interview with Italian Defence Minister Virginio Rognoni in *La Repubblica*, 31 October 1991.
53. Note 3.
54. Ibid.
55. *Die Welt*, 29 October 1991.
56. To appreciate the depth of German dissatisfaction on this issue, see *Welt am Sonntag* (Hamburg), 27 October 1991.
57. *Jane's Defence Weekly*, 30 November 1991, p.1031.
58. The United States agreed to support the Allied Rapid Reaction Corps with an undetermined number of aircraft at the May 1991 NATO Defense Planning Committee meeting; see *Washington Post*, 24 May 1991.
59. The *Bundeswehr*, for instance, does not have the logistical transportation, let alone to date, command capabilities to support any sizeable deployment of forces beyond Germany's borders. See Dirk Sommer's piece in *Europaeische Sicherheit* (Herford), April 1991, pp.234–239.

Peacekeeping in the New Europe

JAMES E. GOODBY

Events in eastern Europe since 1989 have proved that the use of military force is no less unthinkable in the new Europe than it was during the depths of the cold war. Yugoslavia has disintegrated into chaos and civil war. Military force has been deployed and sometimes used in several cities of the former Soviet Union, including Moscow. Ethnic claims and quarrels have erupted in the Czech and Slovak Republic. Romania and Bulgaria are wrestling with problems of minorities that threaten a breakdown in public order. Indeed, one may ask whether the contradiction between order and justice in central and eastern Europe is so profound that the post-cold war era will be more conflict-ridden than the enforced stability of the past 40 years. Could it be that violence will become more commonplace and more intense than during the cold war?

Predictions of cataclysms beyond any known since World War II may be off the mark since state-to-state conflict seems very unlikely. Violence will certainly occur, since internal instabilities are likely to persist for at least the next generation in central and eastern Europe, and almost certainly longer. The breakup of Yugoslavia has created conditions that *The Economist* has quite rightly labelled 'war in Europe', and the coup in Moscow came perilously close to precipitating a civil war. Internal battles, however, may be a threat to international peace and security. This was the principle adopted by the UN Security Council in deciding to authorize intervention in Iraq to aid the Kurds. We should consider whether the principle also should be applied to Europe.

Intervention in an internal conflict could lead the nations of Europe to take sides against each other. Although the major powers have shown little interest in having their own military forces become involved in any way in the ethnic or intra-state conflicts of eastern Europe, statements by the pre-coup Soviet government came close to threatening war if other countries, for any reason, decided to intervene in Yugoslavia.

We should also understand that neither NATO nor the European Community can be counted on to provide a stable haven for the central and eastern Europe countries for quite a time to come. This means that that region will continue to exist in a kind of limbo, while, still further to the east, the construction of a post-Communist order in the former Soviet Union will no doubt be a spectacularly disorderly process. This is the kind of environment that balance-of-power theorists and practical politicians alike can be hardly be faulted for seeing as a temptation to fate. It is hard to escape the conclusion that central and eastern Europe will remain relatively unstable and that incidents may occur there which will invite the use of military force. Yugoslavia has already demonstrated this point. How can such conflicts be prevented, contained, or resolved? Is there a role for the collective authorization and use of military force in dealing with such incidents? Should the United States become involved? These are the key questions in considering the use of force in the new Europe.

Intervention in civil wars carries great risks and usually should be avoided. International peacekeeping forces may be necessary, however, to help to contain the conflict within the borders of the affected state. Furthermore, if one accepts the dictum that 'all wars must end', it is plausible that some wars might end with all parties asking for peacekeeping forces. In such cases, third-party intervention with military force could be indispensable. The unwillingness of the majority of the states directly concerned with the issue of peaceful change in the Balkans to consider the use of armed peacekeeping forces is quite sensible, but it means that a new world order in Europe ultimately will be lacking one essential precondition.

The conflict, amounting to civil war, in Yugoslavia has established a number of not very encouraging precedents regarding the peaceful settlement of disputes in the new Europe. In November 1990, the heads of states and governments agreed on a document called *The Charter of Paris for a New Europe*. It assigned a major role to the Conference on Security and Co-operation in Europe (CSCE) for keeping the peace in Europe. From the beginning of the armed conflict in late June, however, when Slovenia and Croatia declared their independence, the CSCE has played a marginal role. The new CSCE mechanism for the peaceful settlement of disputes, outlined at an experts' meeting in Valletta in February 1991, was adopted by the CSCE Council of Ministers in June 1991 and endowed with a set of procedures for activating the mechanism. This included the ability to call a meeting if roughly one-third of the members of the CSCE requested one. Despite this, the CSCE has not been used in any significant way as a means of settling disputes.

Instead, the European Community has invented a new dispute-settlement mechanism. A peace conference chaired by Lord Carrington, the former British Foreign Secretary and NATO Secretary General, sought to negotiate differences between the conflicting parties. The peace conference, which met for the first time on 7 September 1991 in The Hague, included the leaders of Yugoslavia's six republics, the eight-member collective Yugoslav presidency, and EC ministers. Those issues that are not resolved by negotiation would be handed to a five-member arbitration board whose decisions would be binding. The five members would be the heads of constitutional courts in France, Italy and Germany, plus one judge from Croatia and Serbia. The board would be required to reach a decision within two months after Lord Carrington submitted a case to it.

This action is likely to undermine the CSCE mechanism for the settling of disputes, perhaps damaging permanently the prospects for a European peacekeeping operation that would include the United States and Russia. There are many reasons for this outcome. Soviet opposition to a peacekeeping role for the CSCE in Yugoslavia has been cited above. The aspirations of France and other European nations for a defence and foreign policy agenda for the European Community help to explain their preference for the EC over the CSCE. The unanimity rule in the CSCE would give Yugoslavia a veto over any decision in that body, thus suggesting that other institutions might better handle the peacekeeping function in Europe. As for the United States, which has a major stake in heading off conflict in Europe, the Bush administration has been quite content to leave the problem in the hands of the European Community.

The CSCE has been tangentially involved in one important aspect of peacekeeping in Yugoslavia: the provisions of unarmed observers to monitor cease-fire agreements. At a meeting in Prague on 8-9 August 1991, the CSCE's Committee of Senior Officials, with Yugoslavia concurring, agreed to include other CSCE participating states invited by Yugoslavia in the observation teams. Yugoslavia thus agreed to accept observers from the Czech and Slovak Republic, Poland, Sweden and Canada. The Committee of Senior Officials also agreed to hold further meetings on the crisis in Yugoslavia and to provide good offices for meditation.

But in the main it has been the European Community that has borne the burden of working for cease-fires, fielding observers, and searching for formulas to get negotiations started between Croatia and Serbia. Ever since early July this burden occupied a large part of the time of the Dutch Foreign Minister, who was also the President of the EC Council of Ministers during the latter part of 1991. EC mediation was fairly successful in the case of Slovenia. The Community negotiated an agreement that called for the federal Yugoslav army to return to barracks in both Slovenia and Croatia and for the two republics to suspend for three months their declarations of independence of 25 June 1991. The agreement was carried out in Slovenia, including EC observers being dispatched there, but not in Croatia, where over 11 per cent of the population is Serbian.

Efforts made by the Community's emissaries to Yugoslavia – the foreign ministers of the countries providing the previous, present, and next presidencies of the Council of Ministers – have been intensive and ingenious – and have, by and large, been ignored by Serbia. In addition to proposing that foreign observers be sent to Croatia to observe a cease-fire, the EC has threatened economic sanctions, and individual EC members have said they may recognize Croatian independence. The EC has refused to send observers to areas where a cease-fire had not taken hold.

The one peacekeeping method that had not been tried as of mid-September 1991 is that of sending armed peacekeeping units to Croatia to defend both Serbs and Croats. There has been some public discussion of it but nothing more. On 19 September, the Community foreign ministers considered a Dutch suggestion for organizing an armed peacekeeping force. France, Germany, and Italy supported the idea but Britain strongly opposed it, citing its own experience in Northern Ireland. The idea was dropped in favour of strenghtening a 200-man civilian observer force.

John Tagliabue, the perceptive Balkans correspondent of the *New York Times*, summed up the situation as of 15 September 1991:

> . . . efforts to establish a cease-fire, despite the presence of dozens of cease-fire monitors operating under the flag of the community, were failing miserably . . . the little war was increasingly becoming a test of the effectiveness of forging a common European foreign policy in a post-cold war world. With ethnic rivalries and nationalist conflicts like those in Yugoslavia abounding throughout newly democratic central Europe, the test was not going well at all.[1]

The European Community cannot bear all the blame for this situation. None of the European institutions that might be able to dispose of armed peacekeeping forces could, in fact, plausibly be used for this purpose. The EC, through its potential military arm, the Western European Union (WEU), may be moving in that direction, but obviously there are serious reservations within the Community. The revolution of August 1991 in the Soviet Union may have made it easier to use NATO for peacekeeping purposes. This is still a dubious proposition, however, because several NATO members will prefer to use the EC for peacekeeping tasks, while others will be reluctant to act at all.

The UN might be a possible sponsor of peacekeeping operations in eastern Europe, since the key members of the UN Security Council in such instances would be the United States, Russia, France, and the United Kingdom, each directly concerned with European security issues. A key European nation would be omitted from the decision-making process in the Security Council; however, Germany clearly would be crucial in any effort to mount peacekeeping operations in eastern Europe, even if her forces were not to be used direct. The USSR was reluctant to authorize the use of force to deal with the situation in Yugoslavia, but developments since the August coup attempt will have removed the main reason for that objection, which was fear of outside intervention in the Baltic states.

It is obvious that the CSCE, a process recently endowed with institutions designed to promote peace and prevent conflict, has comparatively little capability to deter conflict, to impose sanctions, or to authorize the use of force in peacekeeping operations. The CSCE process has not encompassed even fact-finding and conciliation until recently. The CSCE's new organizations – especially the Council of Ministers, the Committee of Senior Officials, and the Conflict Prevention Centre – have recently been assigned such roles, but procedural delays have been built into their mandate that will diminish their ability to respond promptly to crises. If one believes, as this writer does, that the case of Yugoslavia shows the need for mounting peacekeeping operations – including military forces – in the new Europe, the present deficiencies in the CSCE render it close to useless in dealing with foreseeable contingencies.

As mentioned above, as a result of decisions made in its first meeting in Berlin in June 1991, the Council of Ministers of the CSCE made it possible to convene an emergency meeting of the Committee of Senior Officials if approximately one-third of the participants endorsed the need for it. But decisions of the CSCE that might flow from such emergency meetings are still based on the consensus rule. There is a case to be made for strengthening the CSCE by authorizing peacekeeping operations by a qualified majority vote of the CSCE participants if specific circumstances come into play. The one circumstance that appeals to this writer as justifying a departure from the usual unanimity rule would occur when the disputants in a given situation asked for the applicant of armed peacekeeping operations. This is the same condition that EC members have cited as the *sine qua non* for deployment of EC peacekeeping force. If the CSCE is not capable of adapting to new circumstances it will die, and it is in some danger of doing just that.

The task of the CSCE has been to build what political scientists call a 'regime', the norms and rules of behaviour that states expect themselves and others to observe. In the human rights field, the CSCE has been amazingly successful. It has enjoyed some successes also in the area of military transparency and the regulation of force levels. The present question is whether the CSCE can establish processes to deal with threats to peace and security in Europe that stem from internal conflict.

Conciliation, as the EC experience in Yugoslavia shows, is probably an inadequate tool if not backed up by some credible ability to deploy military force. Planning for and, if necessary, getting experience in the use of military forces for peacekeeping purposes will also be an essential part of the 'regime'-building function of the CSCE in dealing with internal conflicts.

There are three types of peacekeeping operation that might be needed and could be feasible even under the rule of unanimity in the CSCE. The reality of these examples has been demonstrated in Yugoslavia. These are:

- use of military or paramilitary units to observe a situation that contains some risk of conflict;
- use of such units to control borders or other sensitive political-military areas; and
- use of such forces to establish buffer zones between opposed military forces.

In each of these cases, it is possible that no objection would be raised by states involved in situations that seemed to threaten conflict. These states might even actively seek such help. Such situations might involve all of the possible crises that one can envisage in eastern Europe: ethnic disputes within one state, political sub-units of one state on the verge of conflict with one another, and two states that are on collision course over some unresolved issue.

The Yugoslav tragedy is replete with questions that must be addressed within the CSCE. What could be done if a state or states and all the factions involved in a dispute asked for peacekeeping forces and one member of the CSCE objected? And what about the case where a state or factions directly involved in a dispute stipulated that troops from certain named countries should not be assigned to peacekeeping duties? Finally, how should CSCE deal with a situation where a state *not* directly involved in a dispute objected to the presence in a peacekeeping operation of forces from another CSCE participant? All of these questions, if brought to the full membership of the CSCE for decision, would have to be settled by the principle of unanimity at present. Any single CSCE participant could prevent or perhaps badly cripple a peacekeeping operation. A change in CSCE decision-making procedures to allow peacekeeping operations to proceed if *all* the parties directly involved requested this will probably be necessary if the CSCE is to become a serious security institution in Europe. In the cases of objections to the inclusion of troops from particular countries in peacekeeping missions, a reasonable approach would be to negotiate the question of the composition of peacekeeping forces as part of the process of organizing these forces in each situation.

Contingency planning in the Conflict Prevention Centre should be authorized so that CSCE participants may consider issues that will have to be decided if military forces are ever to be authorized by them in crises. These include the authority to send and receive forces, the national origins of forces, command arrangements, and readiness status. Resort to military force in post-cold war Europe may occur for a variety of reasons – internal instabilities being the most likely and inter-state power struggles the least. In considering collective responses to military crises, several institutions are potentially available: the UN, the European Community, NATO, the WEU, and the CSCE. Many conceivable contingencies in eastern Europe might be handled best in an all-European framework, of which the CSCE is the only existing element that deals with security.

The involvement of the United States in maintaining peace not only in western Europe but also in central and eastern Europe is probably essential to long-term stability in Europe. The evidence of traditional divergencies of view between Germany, France, and Britain on eastern European issues has been quite clear in the case of Yugoslavia. The CSCE gives the United States an institutionalized voice on all European issues and provides a fulcrum for the weight of the United States to lever Europe from indecision to action. Priority attention, therefore, must be assigned to the task of giving the CSCE peacekeeping functions and capabilities.

NOTES

1. John Tagliabue, 'Croatia's Dying Dream', *New York Times*, 15 September 1991, Section 4, p. E2.

The Emerging European Arms Control Arena

JOSEPH F. PILAT

The 'Revolutions of 1989' that resulted in the unification of Germany, the end of Soviet domination in eastern and central Europe, the demise of the Warsaw Pact, and the internal disintegration of the Soviet Union have irrevocably transformed East–West relations. The East–West military confrontation that has dominated the European and global strategic landscape since 1945 has declined so precipitately that even the terms 'East' and 'West' no longer appear meaningful. The cold war is over, the old Europe of rival military blocs is dead. In this new European security environment, the old arms control agenda, which was developed in the context of East–West military confrontation in Europe, has increasingly been questioned.

The Conventional Forces in Europe (CFE) Treaty, signed in Paris on 19 November 1990, marks the end of an era. The CFE mandate was designed to create a quantitative balance between the conventional armed forces of the Atlantic Alliance and of the Warsaw Pact: at the present time, the Pact and the threat it posed have disappeared and the parties to the CFE have other priorities. CFE negotiations began before the scope of change in Europe was fully evident. When it became clear that the European security environment had dramatically changed, there were debates over whether it would be useful to continue the negotiations on CFE. At that time, however, the political rationale for CFE was still compelling to all participating states, and it was argued that the treaty would offer military advantages as well.

After the treaty was concluded, Soviet behaviour, including an attempt to exempt *matériel* from the Treaty's coverage and great shifts of treaty-limited items east of the Urals, outside the area covered by CFE, resulted in further negotiations and political debates. After these were concluded favourably, it was assumed that the Treaty would be ratified and implemented. With the disintegration of the Soviet Union, the Treaty's effective implementation is no longer certain, as differences between the republics threaten to unravel the provisions of CFE. The new Commonwealth of Independent States has an uncertain future, but it could provide a framework in which to proceed with CFE implementation. In any event, both the political and the security interests of the parties suggest that ways will be found to bring the treaty into force. Obviously the CFE Treaty, even if fully implemented, may end an era but is not a finale.

At the Paris Summit in November 1990, the leaders of the states participating in the Conference on Security and Co-operation in Europe (CSCE) agreed to a future arms control agenda that included both the resumption of the CFE and confidence- and security-building measures (CSBM) negotiations, and the creation of a new arms control forum after the Helsinki CSCE Review Conference in the spring of 1992. In addition, there was a US–Soviet commitment to negotiations on short-range nuclear forces (SNF) following the conclusion of the CFE Treaty.

At present, the dramatic initiative of President Bush on unilateral arms reductions, presented in a speech on 27 September 1991, and then President Gorbachev's positive response, appears to preclude the need for SNF negotiations. If implemented, those unilateral, reciprocal actions will remove all land-based SNF from Europe. The CFE and CSBM follow-on negotiations have been underway, but developments in the old Soviet Union could jeopardize them as questions of diplomatic representation and other issues are raised within the Commonwealth. The so-called CFE IA, which is addressing manpower limitations and aerial inspections, and, perhaps, one or more stabilizing measures, began in earnest following the resolution in June 1991 of Soviet efforts to reinterpret certain elements of the CFE Treaty. CSBM negotiations are continuing, with a number of modest proposals under consideration. And the Open Skies negotiations, which broke down in 1990, resumed in 1991. After major concessions by other states, the Soviet Union finally agreed to open all of its territory to overflights, making the conclusion of an agreement possible by the time of the Helsinki Review Conference.

As this activity, on-going and promised, suggests, arms control is certain to continue to be an important feature of European security. Not everything on the old agenda may be considered as completed, especially if there are difficulties in fully implementing the CFE Treaty. But, even if the Treaty is fully implemented, forces in the territory of the old Soviet Union are likely to remain for some time the largest in Europe. The political considerations that drove the CFE negotiations to a conclusion after their original purpose was obviated by the changes in the East are still powerful, as was evidenced by the formulation of a follow-on arms control agenda and by the reopening of Open Skies negotiations. Indeed, as the east Europeans strive to guarantee their security in a dangerous world, and all Europeans seek to establish a new European security architecture, the political force of arms control may even have become more significant. The search for a new arms control agenda to further security and stability will be taken up in Helsinki; the search, undertaken in the setting of a dynamic world with newly-emerging threats, among more participants with a great diversity of interests, will be far more difficult than previously was the case.

Before looking forward, it is essential to evaluate the past, specificially the CFE Treaty, which if it had been concluded only two years earlier would have universally been regarded as historic, and as resolving the most essential Western security issues in Europe. On the assumption that the Treaty will fully be in force, what assessments of the Treaty's impact on European security can at present be given?

The CFE Treaty was clearly not in the forefront of the changes that resculpted the face of Europe. Arms control has lagged behind political change. It has reacted to or ignored, rather than guided, change. Indeed, the changes in Europe fostered achievements far more important for the realization of the Treaty's mandate – to establish a stable and secure balance of conventional forces at lower levels, to eliminate disparities in forces, and to eliminate the capability to launch a surprise attack and to initiate large-scale offensive action – than the Treaty itself. Yet, even though the Treaty was the cart rather than the horse in the changes sweeping Europe, its implementation will probably bring significant benefits. Its conclusion has contributed to the emerging new environment, fostering a sense of security among the European publics, particularly in the emerging east European democracies. But it should have more concrete benefits. One is to regulate change and make desired changes more difficult to reverse. Another is to improve predictability in the assessment of future threats in the Atlantic-to-the-Urals region, and, thereby, in principle, in warning time, on the basis of which the United States and its allies could respond to unfavourable changes.

In this context, CFE has or will help to ensure and further positive developments. The CFE negotiations, even before the Treaty was concluded, provided a framework for the realization of German unification and the limitation of German military forces in a manner that met both Soviet and German security concerns. The framework was, in this case, necessary but not sufficient. It must be recognized that the 'two plus four' talks were crucial for the achievement of unification, and that to avoid an unacceptable 'singularization' of Germany, CFE IA is designed to impose limits on the military manpower of the other CFE parties.

The negotiations also served to promote east Europe's independence. To be sure, the negotiations involved 'groups of states', i.e., NATO and the Warsaw Treaty Organization (WTO); however, as the WTO was becoming more and more obsolete, the east European states were able to negotiate as individual states within their group and with the West. Further, the Treaty's rights and obligations (including those involving inspections) apply to individual states, and the Treaty allows no stationing of foreign forces on the territory of a party without its permission.

The Treaty itself, when fully implemented, will have substantial benefits. It will result in the destruction or conversion of large quantities of treaty-limited equipment. It will place significant limits on the forces allowed in the territory of the old Soviet Union west of the Urals, especially through the sufficiency rule and the manner in which it has been implemented to date – negotiations among the former WTO states resulted in fewer entitlements for the Soviet Union. For example, the 13,300 tanks that the sufficiency rule would have allowed the Soviet Union, after reductions mandated by the Treaty have been reduced to 13,150. Negotiations between Russia and the other republics within the Atlantic-to-the-Urals region over the distribution of force entitlements could be controversial and threaten the Treaty's implementation, but they could also provide a framework for future stability in this area. As suggested, the new Commonwealth may provide a framework for the resolution of any differences over entitlements, although the discussions on conventional forces are proving to be difficult and may be protracted.

The Treaty will also facilitate transparency with respect to the structure, size, and disposition of conventional armed forces in Europe, in conjunction with agreed CSBMs, through stabilizing measures and an elaborate verification regime. While this regime is very intensive in certain of its aspects, it is more a confidence-building measure than a traditional verification regime. It is clear, however, that the Treaty's verification provisions will enhance the national intelligence measures of the parties, especially its detailed provisions for information exchange, on-site inspections, challenge inspections, and on-site observation of equipment destruction.

And, because of its force limitations and its promotion of openness, transparency, and predictability, the Treaty will enable the West to adjust its forces and strategy to reflect the new conditions on the continent without undermining its security. Even if, as can be expected, political and budgetary pressures lead the West to reduce forces below the baselines established by the Treaty, such choices should be less dangerous now with the Treaty than if it did not exist. It would appear, then, that the treaty will continue to have military as well as political significance, even with the changes in eastern and central Europe that have obviated its original objectives. But, despite these benefits, it is not a very useful model for future arms control in Europe.

NEW THREATS; NEW ARMS CONTROL APPROACHES

CFE had been for the West, before the 'Revolutions of 1989', a clear objective. There was among the Western allies a consensus, relatively speaking, on the old threat posed by the Soviet Union and the Warsaw Pact, and the political, military, and arms control approaches adopted to deal with that threat. In the arms control arena, the approach envisaged quantitative reductions to rectify massive NATO–WTO force imbalances, and this was the central feature of CFE.

With the demise of the Soviet Union, threats to European security remain, but there will be no future threats of the same magnitude. Those threats that will most likely appear, seen from the vantage of the present, derive primarily from the East and the South. The resurgence of Russia or other hostile Soviet successor states, with the possibility of multiple centres of nuclear weapons on the former territory of the Soviet Union, is a primary concern. As well, there is a real prospect of serious destabilization due to problems with Soviet nuclear weapon surety; the economic and political collapse in the old Soviet Union and perhaps eastern Europe; the breakdown of the democratization process in eastern Europe, with the possible return to authoritarian regimes and great migrations of refugees to the West; and the prospect of ethnic warfare and civil war in the Balkans and the old Soviet Union, with the breakdown of order in Yugoslavia as a model. In addition, the proliferation of weapons of mass destruction and out-of-area conflicts could have grave consequences for the security interests of the United States and its allies, or for the states of eastern Europe and the former Soviet Union. Indeed, such threats, especially such proliferation on Europe's southern and eastern periphery, could directly undermine European security.

Threats of this nature pose grave dangers to European stability and security, and could disrupt the search for a new security architecture. Such threats will inevitably be ambiguous, with the possible exception of resurgent Russia, over which there might be a new consensus in the West. It is, however, difficult to imagine a Western consensus on most threats, at least on concrete responses, and particularly when arms control proposals and military reactions are involved. And, even to the extent that a consensus might develop, these threats are less responsive to traditional arms control approaches. The problems of force reconstitution and of an attack following mobilization – which appear to be the most important of the post-CFE security contingencies – are not and probably cannot be dealt with in the current arms control agenda.

If old arms control objectives and the current agenda do not address emerging issues and concerns, what are the potential objectives and the agenda for arms control in Europe? Potential arms control objectives include both items from the old agenda that were not completed, and entirely new items.

The primary issue left on the old agenda is that of further reductions of existing conventional armed forces. Whether they remain unified or are divided among the republics, the conventional forces on the territory of the old Soviet Union will be the largest in Europe. Their reduction and restructuring will be of interest to all the CFE parties. The economies of the republics are in dire straits, and may be expected to result in force levels lower than the republics' entitlements. However, economic concerns are likely to ensure that any such reductions will not be subjected to expensive destruction processes, and there are severe limits to economically-viable conversion. As a consequence, vast quantities of armaments will probably remain in the old Soviet Union west of the Urals during a protracted time of transition. Further reductions of Western forces are also likely, and formal provisions for further cuts could have appeal as 'sanctioning' budget-driven reductions in the West.

Ultimately, however, further formal reductions will be difficult in a rapidly changing security environment, and are unlikely to receive the priority accorded to economic and political, as well as to other security issues, such as attempts to address the issues of force structure, military doctrine, force reconstitution and defence conversion, and defence budgets, which are certain to be discussed as any future agenda is being formulated. All of these issues, and others, may best be addressed by two approaches likely to be on the new agenda: the development of measures to promote transparency, predictability, and openness or merely dialogue on some matters; and the seeking of a framework for 'ratifying' unilateral, perhaps reciprocal, actions, including force reductions.

In addition to these quantitative and qualitative approaches to limiting conventional arms, the future arms control agenda will be defined by a search for a new security architecture in Europe and by threats to European security originating from outside Europe. A new security architecture will have to address the complex of issues suggested by the concept of a 'common European home', including institutions and their relationships. But the most pressing problems are likely to involve sub-regional tensions and conflicts, perhaps only resolvable by mediations, fact-finding, and peace-keeping efforts. The search for means to enhance stability and security in east central and southern Europe, especially in the Balkans, Cyprus, the Mediterranean, east Europe, and the Soviet successor states, will be paramount in this regard. Concerns about problems from within Europe will be heightened by problems from without. While so-called out-of-area contingencies have long been discussed in NATO, little has been done. New challenges, especially from the Middle East, the Persian Gulf, and northern Africa, as well as from the East, may give such contingencies a new urgency. On the agenda, then, will be a search for effective measures and mechanisms to address extra-regional issues, including conventional arms transfers, the proliferation of weapons of mass destruction (nuclear, biological and chemical) and their means of delivery (missiles), terrorism, and drugs.

Before the prospect that SNF might be dealt with through reciprocal, unilateral actions, it strongly appeared that limitations on tactical nuclear weapons would also be an objective in European arms control endeavours. Only air-deliverable nuclear weapons will remain in Europe after the unilateral cuts are put into effect, but there may ultimately be calls to eliminate these weapons totally as well, perhaps through a European nuclear-weapon-free zone or sub-regional zones (e.g., Nordic or Balkan). Furthermore, a long-standing interest in naval arms control could be raised as an objective of arms control, although negotiated naval restrictions have not been viewed as being in Western interests. It is unlikely that either of these issues will attain the priority accorded to others, or that their absence from the agenda would disrupt the consideration of matters with higher priority.

Given these objectives, what is likely to be done?

WHAT IS TO BE DONE?

In the light of current threat perceptions, budgetary constraints, and domestic political priorities throughout the CSCE states, force reductions going beyond, perhaps far beyond, those required by the CFE Treaty are likely. The best approach may be that put forward in recent Bush–Gorbachev nuclear-weapon reduction initatives, that is, unilateral, reciprocal actions. Such an approach will necessarily be more difficult in a multilateral context, and we will, of course, need to monitor the fate of those initiatives. Nonetheless, the approach appears promising. It may be pursued on a timely basis, without the burdens associated with formal negotiations. Indeed, formal negotiations could for a time impede meaningful reductions. Even after the abortive coup and the formation of the Commonwealth, the military in the old Soviet Union seems unlikely to be subjected by political leadership to greater formal reductions. As political battles increase between and among the republics, the military will be seen as an important ally to the contenders for power. Even if deeper reductions occur, whether unilaterally or through formal negotiations, they raise thorny force-planning, readiness, and mobilization issues. Deep cuts do not by themselves resolve the critical future security problem of a reinforced attack, that is, an attack following mobilization.

Formal negotiations may not now provide the best approach to quantitative force reductions; they have never been an appropriate forum for dealing with qualitative issues, such as readiness, nor for addressing the issues of mobilization, conversion of military capabilities to the civilian sphere, or force reconstitution. Any attempts to create restrictions in these areas would generate important problems for American and Western security postures, which will depend on technological (qualitative) superiority, mobilization, and force reconstitution to meet future threats.

If the size and other indices of conventional force strength do not appear promising items for arms control approaches other than unilateral reductions, this reflects the post-CFE security environment. In this there is considerable scope for information exchanges, technical assistance, and the like, regarding military budgets, doctrines, and force structure. To the extent that such modest actions do promote openness and transparency, and thereby reduce tensions and insecurities, they could actually address the heart of current problems, although they are by their very nature limited and primarily useful in so far as the largely positive trends of the present time continue.

Neither sub-regional issues, such as Cyprus, or extra-regional issues, including Middle East and Persian Gulf security after the Gulf War, appear susceptible to any but the most modest confidence-building measures in the foreseeable future, although even modest CBMs could be useful. Such issues remain divisive in European and Atlantic councils, and have long been a bane to formal arms control agreements. As experience in Yugoslavia and during the Gulf War appears to indicate, these issues are not yet ripe for harvest.

A host of confidence-building measures and unilateral actions (reciprocal and co-ordinated), from mere dialogue on unresolvable issues to unilateral deep cuts in some areas of conventional forces in Europe, are all possible and would seem to be the best possible approach to outstanding issues confronting European security. The prospect for Open Skies in the new, post-coup climate is a startling demonstration of what is now possible. For the last year, traditional Soviet concerns about security and secrecy resulted in a stalemate in the considerations of a proposal genuinely perceived by all other states involved (save one) to be in their mutual interest. After the coup, the stronger opponents of Open Skies have been discredited or witnessed their influence in relative decline. The regime on which we are likely to reach agreement will not be as useful as the one that had been hoped for in terms of the number of overflights and the quality of information received (which is closely tied to the confidence-building function). However, a regime will probably be created and have a possibility of developing over time. What was critical in the anticipated success, other than the Soviet reversal, was the political imperative for transparency, even if it will be largely symbolic.

However the arms agenda develops, the new issues, and probably old ones as well, will be discussed in multiple forums, existing and yet to be created. The ongoing CFE and CSBM follow-on negotiations, along with the restarted Open Skies negotiations, are crucial in the near term, especially as a means of dealing with issues remaining from the old agenda (CFE IA) and furthering the process of building openness and transparency (CSBMs and Open Skies). All of these forums, however, are likely to be closed, to fade away, or to be incorporated into the post-Helsinki arms control forum. This has yet to be created and its mandate talks, set to begin at the Helsinki Review Conference in 1992, may be extraordinarily difficult owing to the rapidly changing European security environment, as well as the divergent security interests of as many as 49 or more states.

The CSCE and its new institutional structures, especially the Conflict Prevention Centre (CPC), will provide forums for addressing security concerns. There is widespread interest in strengthening and redefining the CPC and other structures to enable them to conduct fact-finding, mediation, and peacekeeping missions effectively, and to provide a framework for dialogue on military forces, defence budgets, and, perhaps, extraregional contingencies. And, perhaps, other new vehicles for addressing and managing changes in military forces, doctrines, and security policy will be found that do not bear any old institutional burdens of having been designed for, and in, the cold war security context, and are able to respond directly to the current projected needs of the new arms control agenda.

CONCLUSIONS

Activities in any forum will not produce a grandiose CFE II; there are unlikely to be further formalized quantitative reductions or new qualitative reductions. The addressing of qualitative issues may be appealing to many states, but, as indicated, it is impracticable and cuts against Western interests, which will continue to depend on qualitative superiority in the military sphere to ensure that the global interests of the United States, its friends and its allies are protected. If the goal is security and stability in Europe, the promotion of openness and transparency through multiple endeavours, rather than through further quantitative (or qualitative) limitations on conventional forces, appears to deserve the highest priority by policy makers.

The Latest Stage of the German Question:
Pax Germanica in the New Europe

ANDREI S. MARKOVITS AND SIMON REICH

INTRODUCTION

To call 1989 an *annus mirabilis* might almost be an understatement. That year, much like 1618, 1776, 1789, 1918 or 1945, represents one of those rare turning points which have altered the course of global history. If one defines a revolution as a fundamental reorganization of existing power relations in state and society, a change in elites, the complete redefinition of private and public, as well as the introduction of a new economic order, then surely the events in Hungary, Czechoslovakia, Poland, the German Democratic Republic, Yugoslavia, Bulgaria, Albania – Romania being something of an exception – qualified as quintessentially revolutionary. Rather than detract from the enormity of these revolutions, the fact that, with Romania's and Yugoslavia's exception, they occurred without violence, further enhances their importance.

As in the case of most revolutions, the ramifications of the revolutions of 1989 went well beyond their domestic confines, profoundly affecting the international order. Coupled with the implosion of the Soviet Union, 1989 witnessed the demise of the world system established in Yalta and Potsdam in 1945. Globally, the Soviet Union and its successor states ceased to be America's equal as a superpower. Yet, instead of returning to the days of the *Pax Americana* of the immediate postwar settlement, when the United States was the unchallenged power in the world, we seem to be drifting towards an age of multipolarity where – at least in the important realms of the economy, science and technology – Europe and Japan are poised to become at least America's equals. The events of 1989 restored Europe to its pre-1945 entity by allowing a relegated and long-forgotten eastern Europe to join its integrating partners in the West. Thus, perhaps more than even the vaunted '1992' – the beginning of the European Internal Market – 1989 can justly claim to be the year of Europe. It most certainly can claim to be Germany's year. With the fall of the Berlin Wall on 9 November, it was only a matter of time before the two Germanys would once again become one. The unification of the two Germanys and the two Berlins meant the definitive end of the two Europes – at least in its 'cold war' dimension.

TRADITIONAL DEBATES IN NEW CONTEXTS

In the context of these events, Germany's unification engendered the emergence of a new stage of the 'German question' that has dominated modern European political, economic and military relations for over a century. The traditional formulation of this *problematique* has always started from the working assumption that Germany's elites have sought to expand their economic and territorial base beyond their universally-defined geographic borders. Such motives were assigned to Germany's leadership from Bismarck to Hitler. The corresponding, responsive role of the other major European powers was always to constrain this purposive, imperialist behaviour – either through alliances designed to balance German power in the period before 1945, or through multilateral institutions, such as NATO and the European Community (EC), designed to co-opt Germany in the postwar period. Germany has therefore been, at worst, a traditional adversary and, at best, an un-reliable ally.

In the period before 1945 Germany's imperialist ambitions were always ultimately subdued by the constraint imposed by its domestic resource base. The country lacked the ultimate capacity to predominate in a long military struggle against its neighbours because it could not muster superior logistical capabilities. In the postwar period such a strategy was never even contemplated, as Germany's leaders imbued with a profound sense of their country's culpable past and self-imposed, strictly-defined limitations on its future role, were content to subordinate any expansionist tendencies to trading concerns. This latter tendency was encapsulated in the description of Germany as an 'economic giant and a political dwarf'.

Now academics of all hues and colours are debating Germany's current role in the new Europe. They contest the issue of whether Germany's unification, given the end of bipolarity, will lead to Germany's expansion. Typically, academics on the whole continue to be generally divided along the traditional lines defined by the formulation of the 'German question' for over a century. They therefore argue about whether Germany's elites are likely to pursue with purpose imperialist economic, political and – in the vision of the most alarmist observers – even military policies in the new Europe. We begin by offering a summary of this debate.

The Optimists' View

Arguments stressing the benign effect of German unification for European security and economic development reflect one of three critical elements. Although they might combine aspects of more than one form, this intellectual approach is preponderantly functional, institutional or sociological. Whichever form the argument takes, it tends to focus on postwar history for supporting evidence.

The first argument involves an extension of the functional approach used by integration theory so traditionally popular among scholars studying the development of the EC.[1] In this context the argument focuses on the taming of German power and influence through the country's involvement in international organizations, such as the EC and NATO. There are at least two assumptions behind this approach. The first is that involvement in such institutions has bred a series of interdependent rather than dominant relationships between Germany and its partners that are likely to promote friendship rather than friction. This assumption lay behind the initial American promotion of Franco–German collaboration, dating back to the early 1950s.[2] The product is a Germany 'tamed' by its international ties. Wolfram Hanrieder identifies this functional component as part of America's postwar 'double containment' policy against Germany and the Soviet Union.[3] Moreover, its proponents would presumably suggest, in extending this logic, that just as a policy of military containment successfully constrained Soviet aggression, so it will continue to limit any German imperialist ambitions. The second assumption is that states are interested in absolute rather than relative gains, and that Germany's trading arrangements with its partners are positive-sum in effect, that is that they are of mutual benefit to both.[4] On the basis of this assumption, the hope is that the primary effect of Germany's involvement in organizations like the EC will be that Germany's economic strength will allow it to act as a locomotive for broader European development as its foreign trade and investment grow. Helmut Kohl has himself been a major advocate of this view.[5] This claim is open to empirical verification. At this point we simply stress that this view suggests that successful German development can only occur within the context of broad European growth.

The second, institutional argument supporting a benign image of the effects of German unification focuses on the postwar development of Germany's domestic political system. Josef Joffe has been a particularly vocal proponent of this view. Joffe essentially interprets and then extends the argument first developed by Peter Katzenstein in *Policy and Politics in West Germany: the Growth of a Semi-Sovereign State*, where Katzenstein suggests that postwar institutional reforms have fragmented the German state and resulted in a 'taming' of its capacities.[6] Joffe points to the acceptance of a system of federalism and democratic values as the political structure of the new Germany assimilates that of the old Federal Republic. He then invokes this image of a tamed German state to suggest that Germany's foreign policy will foreswear dominance through either economic imperialism or military aggression as an objective or a product. Domestic democratic reforms, in Joffe's view, will therefore temper German foreign policies.[7] Presumably the evidence in support of such a claim is not only the broadly held view that democracies (such as contemporary Germany) do not start wars, but the more specific German pattern of postwar development in which the *Junker* class – according to Alexander Gerschenkron, the social and economic carrier of German imperialism – was destroyed by Soviet tanks.[8] So, consistent with the conventional view of historians and political scientists, the new united Germany, according to this logic, can be analytically divorced from the history of the old united Germany.[9] The institutionalist argument complements its functionalist equivalent in terms of its view of the benign effect of German unification for the rest of Europe. The principle difference lies in which factors are stressed; the former emphasizes internal constraints on German dominance, while the latter emphasizes its external counterparts.

   The third form is a sociological argument about the evolution of Germany's elites. Its central premise is, in fact, an evolutionary one based on the notion of 'knowledge through learning'. It suggests that German economic, intellectual and political elites are aware of their responsibility for past events and stand vigil, guarding against the re-emergence of militarist, anti-liberal, xenophobic tendencies. This view further argues that Germans feel ambivalent about unification, and retain a deep concern about avoiding their past mistakes. In broad historical terms, the new German political and economic elites represent the postwar triumph of the bourgeoisie and its values over the traditionally imperialist and aggressive behaviour embodied in the agricultural, aristocratic *Junkers* before 1945. These bourgeois values stress a cosmopolitan culture within a European economy where Germany and its trading partners benefit by Germany's emphasis on the advantages of free trade within an export-oriented economy. As a result of this export-orientation, Germany's new economic elites recognize the country's sustained dependence on the willingness of foreigners to buy German goods, and therefore advocate policies that enhance free trade. Germany's political elite is cognizant of the fact that such policies can only be implemented in an environment that emphasizes reconciliation and mutual trust.

   Advocates of this interpretation of Germany's new political elite would typically point to supporting evidence of the type provided by the speech of the German President, Richard von Weizsäcker in May 1985, marking the fortieth anniversary of German capitulation. He supposedly reflected a broad German concern when he stated that 'anyone who closes his eyes to the past is blind to the present. Whoever refuses to remember the inhumanity is prone to the risks of new infection.'[10] Weizsäcker has become the conscience of the new Germany, the fine conservative who admits to the singular evils committed by the Nazis in the name of Germany. Some have cynically referred to him as a 'one-man act of contrition'.

Perhaps more significant than the President's keen awareness of Germany's past is the profound westernization of the Federal Republic's business elite. The cosmopolitan and bourgeois character of West Germany's captains of industry represents perhaps one of the most fundamental differences between the Weimar and the Bonn Republic. In the former, the business class as a whole adhered to a sense of hypernationalism, was profoundly authoritarian, detested the republic's democratic institutions and tried to cow labour by destroying its independence.[11] In marked contrast, Bonn's business elite has been international in outlook and education, has accepted and supported the republic's democratic order, and entered into intricate 'corporatist' arrangements with labour as a fully-accepted junior partner in *Modell Deutschland's* quest to become export champions of the world, a goal attained by 1988. While there have been recent reports of some businessmen, politicians, and academics refusing to conduct interviews in English in the wake of Germany's newly won importance, this German neo-parochialism seems destined to remain relegated to a small but growing fringe in the Federal Republic's public debate.[12]

The Pessimists' View

The pessimists' anguish concerning prospective German hegemony in the light of Germany's unification and the vacuum in Europe created by American and Soviet withdrawal takes two primary forms – one historical, the other cultural. In different ways, both rely on evidence that predates 1945. The historical analysis stresses the notorious aspects of German development dating from unification to the fascist period. It tends to decry the claims of traditional conservative historians that German culpability for the outbreak of two World Wars was limited. Instead it stresses the violent nature of the first German unification, the unsuccessful development of a German bourgeoisie, and therefore the lack of a democratic tradition in explaining not only aggressive foreign policies but the emergence of the necessary antecedent conditions for the Holocaust itself.[13] Indeed, pessimists point to the recent attempts by conservative historians to 'relativize' German policies *vis-à-vis* the Holocaust in the *Historikerstreit* debates as timely supportive evidence of the revisionist tendencies among conservative historians, who reflect a

continuity with their intellectual forebears in their defence of nineteenth-
and early twentieth-century German militarism.[14]

Advocates of this historical approach point to one pattern which they
see as an unerring truth – that Germany's domestic problems have always
been Europe's. The dominant way of compensating for Germany's
internal conflicts has traditionally been through state policies designed to
assist German economic and/or military expansion, whether those
problems consisted of labour or raw material shortages, or simply as a
way of disguising German domestic social turmoil by invoking a
belligerent form of a nationalist spirit.[15] The discussions between
politicians and bureaucrats sponsored by the then Thatcher government
in 1989, and the subsequent 'Chequers Pronouncement' after those
discussions, reflected just such British concerns about the possibility of
renewed German expansionism.[16] Advocates of such an approach point
to the multiple problems Germany faces in integrating the destitute East
German population as one source of potential conflict. They also note as
evidence that one of Kohl's first acts when faced with the realistic
prospect of unification was to cause a dispute about the legitimacy of
Poland's postwar border with East Germany. Although Kohl recognized
that the international uproar generated by his comments threatened to
stall the unification negotiations, leading him to withdraw his claims,
critics noted that Kohl's motive was to attract the electoral support of
right-wing refugees from the former-German territories. This pattern of
'spill-over' – whereby German domestic political conflict is expressed
through an expansionist foreign policy – is an enduring characteristic of
Germany first comprehensively characterized in the imperialist ideology
of *Weltpolitik* of the Wilhelmine. *Weltpolitik* propagated a nationalist
belief that domestic security was contingent upon territorial expansion
and thereby quelled a series of potential social and class conflicts that
otherwise might have erupted into civil strife. Revisionist historians in the
late twentieth century contend that such domestic turmoil and the result-
ing nationalist ideology generated German policies which caused the
outbreak of the First World War.[17]

One should note that this historical approach is also largely structural;
the axiomatic notion that Germany's problems are Europe's because of
Germany's size, power and geographic location means that its European
neighbours must always be concerned about Germany's domestic and
foreign policies. Such a cautionary historical view was recently reflected
in the statement by one Conservative Member of the British Parliament
who reportedly complained about Germany's efforts to secure EC
recognition of Croatia and Slovenia by his referring to Germany's
purportedly bullying tactics as 'the over-mighty Hun' – a rhetoric reflective

of prewar and wartime conceptions of Germans rather than a contemporary one.[18]

A second pessimistic approach with a greater mass appeal, even if it lacks empirical support, focuses on cultural factors. This approach is much more self-consciously voluntaristic and tends to reflect an *Angst* – both within and outside Germany – about Germany's enhanced power and its new problems with the conjunction of reunification and global transformation. Such concerns have been expressed by German intellectuals such as Günter Grass and Jürgen Habermas, while foreigners have tended to stress the slightest sign of any of the recurrent German nationalist symbols – such as references to the weaknesses of Weimar or the joys of Wagner; to the German *Volk* or to its *Vaterland*.[19] Common to both German intellectuals and foreigners is an unease with the prospect of the reappearance of tendencies for so long submerged and a fear that Germany's new democratic culture will prove illusory.

Like the historical approach, the cultural approach recognizes the ambivalence of Germany's pre-1945 and post-1945 experiences and chooses to emphasize its concern that, freed of superpower constraints, the reunited Germany will reflect old habits. The pessimists' greatest fear, in the early 1990s, is reflected in Hermann Kantorowicz's comment, made in 1931, that 'the new Germany's true foe is the old Germany'.[20]

The debate between optimists and pessimists therefore really focuses on the degree of German centrality in the new European order, as well as the implications for Germany's position in Europe and for global stability. Arguments on both sides stress structural, institutional and cognitive attributes, disagreeing principally on whether Germany's primary links are to the period that predates or postdates 1945. The optimists tend to reflect the assumption that European integration is a positive-sum game where the interests of Germany and its European partners are compatible. It was therefore no surprise to them to hear Helmut Kohl declare, at the first congress of the reunited Christian Democratic Union, that 'for me German unity and European unity are two sides of the same coin . . . in truth we are German patriots and convinced Europeans . . . Europe is our future, Germany our fatherland.'[21] The pessimistic view is best reflected in Margaret Thatcher's riposte that 'it will be up to the rest of us to see that Germany does not dominate. Others of us have powerful voices.'[22]

Our formulations are, of course, only ideal-types. In reality, optimists and pessimists cross-cut in the way that they interweave their arguments. While the optimists tend to be relatively unqualified in their position, pessimists are more ambivalent in recognizing the possible rewards of German unity. What they both share, however, is the assumption that the expansion of German power will largely be determined as a result of a conscious choice by Germany's elites. It is at this point that we turn to our alternative formulation.

AN ALTERNATIVE FORMULATION

We argue that the problem posed concerning the 'German question' in its latest form is novel, not only in the context in which it has developed but in the form that it takes. Indeed, it is in some sense unrecognizable. For the contemporary form inverts this traditional assumption about Germany's relationship with its European neighbours. Whichever version of the traditional argument one adopts, whether *optimistic* or *pessimistic*, one begins with the assumption that German expansion, if it occurs, will be the product of purposive behaviour by Germany's elites. We argue that German hegemony will occur. It will, however, largely be the product of the policies of Germany's neighbours rather than any conscious choices made by its own elites.

Ironically, therefore, while Germany's elites in many respects seek to limit their country's involvement in broader European affairs, its neighbours are consciously pursuing a series of policies which have the effect of enhancing German power. The product of this inversion will be a new German hegemony in Europe – largely already realized in the West and soon to follow in the East. Indeed, the comparative historic, cultural and linguistic advantages that Germany enjoys in eastern Europe relative to its western European rivals will promote its interests there, and thus help to consolidate a pan-European hegemony. Without conscious efforts to achieve hegemony, perhaps even consciously resisting such expansion, the Germans will come to dominate Europe to the degree (if not in the manner and for the same purpose) intended by earlier generations of Germans.

UNDERSTANDING GERMAN HEGEMONY

Traditional neo-realist conceptions of hegemony tend to focus exclusively on structural formulations and are applied at the systemic level on a global scale. Any account that focuses purely on this structural centrality, however, is substantially lacking because it ignores an ideological component essential for explaining Germany's emerging position as the European hegemon. Neo-realist definitions of hegemony rely on two alternative formulations in explaining why weaker states defer to stronger ones. The first, liberal form stresses the role of self-interest. It assumes that hegemons are voluntarily accorded their status by the weak because both parties are concerned only about absolute gains. Indeed, proponents of this view suggest that smaller states often gain relatively more than the hegemon from such arrangements. A second, realist view emphasizes the importance of coercion in explaining why a country is accorded hegemonic status. The weak submit to the strong because they must; the strong give them no choice in the matter. Again, however, like the first, liberal approach, the absolute benefits derived from such arrangements are shared.[23]

Neither such approach, however, adequately captures the situation regarding Germany's developing hegemony with its European neighbours. Here, Germany benefits from the present framework while its major trading partners lose, yet Germany does not enforce this system through force as one would otherwise assume. So why do Germany's neighbours voluntarily submit to such a hegemonic system?

To explain this anomaly we rely on a third definition of hegemony – one developed by Antonio Gramsci – which, unlike its mainstream, purely structural, counterparts stresses the role of ideas. Gramsci distinguishes between *dominio* (domination) which he sees as primarily tied to the 'political society's' (i.e., the state's) mechanism to exert its power, and *egemonia* (hegemony) which Gramsci associates with the complex web of power and influence exerted by the most prevalent group(s) in 'civil society'.[24] Whereas domination is always associated with coercion, state power, and indeed force, hegemony, to Gramsci, remains consistently identified with equilibrium, persuasion, consolidation and consent.[25] Gramsci's definition of hegemony thus stresses the explanatory importance of ideas – that this voluntary submission by one party to another is predicated on the belief, right or wrong, that all parties (not just the strong) will benefit from the interaction between the weak and the strong, even though it is important to emphasize that they might not recognize this act as submissive, nor may they recognize that the outcome might indeed be a hegemonic relationship.[26]

In the context of Germany's relationship with Europe, the voluntary submission of Germany's neighbours to Germany's predominance may persuasively be explained by this Gramscian formulation in two respects. First, for the countries of western Europe, but even more so for those of eastern Europe, Germany is the capitalist model to emulate, with its combination of free enterprise and social welfarism captured in the concept of the 'social market economy'. When these factors are further coupled with institutionalized labour's and management's involvement in policy making and which together produce high levels of prosperity, the result is *Modell Deutschland*. Alternatives, such as more centrally-planned economies like the French or more *laissez-faire* ones like the American, lack *Modell*

Deutschland's unique combination of high rates of prosperity and a large, impressive 'safety net' achieved through the democratic representation of labour. The first 'ideological' component of hegemony is therefore the desire to emulate the structure of the German model. With this comes an adherence to German principles about how to organize an economy, as well as an accessibility to German advice and guidance in the formation of economic policy.[27]

The second ideological component is the belief that emulation of the German model also requires active trading with the Germans, not only through the import and export of finished products but also through foreign direct investment and joint ventures. This 'positive-sum' assumption is reminiscent of the myth about Ireland's fabled Blarney Stone – that one can only benefit from its medicinal healing powers through direct contact. With perhaps the singular exception of the British (who appear also to have finally succumbed to the belief that greater integration with Germany is desirable since Margaret Thatcher's departure as Prime Minister), no country has voiced substantial concern that it might be subsidizing German prosperity as a result of this process while reaping little in the way of rewards. Indeed, British attitudes have been criticized by other EC members and have traditionally resulted in Britain's political isolation.

The two ideological elements – emulation through replication and through interaction or integration – therefore combine with the structural centrality that would naturally be accorded to Europe's biggest economy and the world's largest exporter to generate a rapidly developing hegemony.

TWO NOTABLE EXAMPLES

We have elsewhere attempted to demonstrate systematically the economic basis for our claims concerning an emerging German hegemony. Thus it would be inappropriate to repeat that litany of economic data here.[28] Rather than focusing on the economic basis for German hegemony, we therefore offer two brief, recent, important examples. These illustrate our claim that the desire of Germany's neighbours to emulate and interact with the FRG provides Germany with a way to influence heavily those neighbours' behaviour.

The first illustration concerns the terms of the recent agreement at Maastricht on European monetary union. In this particular instance the western European states chose to stabilize their currencies through the adoption of a mechanism designed to keep them within a fixed band, with the intention of shifting towards a single currency during the course of the decade.[29] The design of the agreement largely models itself on the structure of the German Bundesbank, while its terms mainly confer monetary sovereignty on the institution itself. The Bundesbank will become, institutionally, Europe's central bank, a role it developed – according to Paul Welfens – in the 1980s, when it assumed both the economic and political leadership of western European monetary policy. Welfens further states that 'political influence over monetary policy in the EC has been biased towards Germany so far. There has been German dominance of monetary policy on the European continent which implied a loss of policy sovereignty for most other countries'.[30] Interestingly, Welfens notes that in the 1980s the EMS was an asymmetrically fixed exchange-rate zone with Germany playing a special, dominant role 'hardly justified by its economic size or by the role of the Deutsche Mark as both a stable domestic currency and a widely used international reserve currency. The Federal Republic of Germany was the centre country of the continental EMS, and the Deutsche Bundesbank dominated monetary policy in the EC while being able – due to successful stabilized intervention that neutralized the effects of exchange rate intervention – to pursue a domestic monetary target'.[31] In other words, the Bundesbank dominated European monetary policy in the 1980s, and this leadership was not purely the product of its structural centrality, but also, increasingly, due to its political influence borne of respect.[32]

What did this German leadership produce? As Welfens himself suggests, 'with parity adjustments not fully compensating for inflation differentials Germany – and other low-inflation countries – obviously enjoyed the benefit of a gradually increasing price competitiveness in the EC which contributed to higher exports and growth along with lower unemployment in Germany'. While he is definitive on that point, Welfens adds, more contentiously and less self-confidently, that these German measures may have partially contributed to higher growth in some other EMS states.[33] The situation may be best summarized by one informed observer who concurred with the view that 'everybody did what they thought was best, and the Germans got exactly what they wanted'.[34]

Soon after the agreement was reached in December 1991, Germany's major European trading partners got a foretaste of the sorts of implications they may expect from this new system when the Bundesbank raised two key interest rates in order to quell inflationary pressures at home – a move which squarely contradicted French and British economic policies and the desires on the part of other Europeans to lower interest rates in order to alleviate domestic recessions.[35]

The second example pertained to EC recognition of Slovenia and Croatia. The recent events in Yugoslavia generated heated discussion among EC officials concerned about stability in eastern Europe. The Germans, of course, have an extensive history of involvement in this region, being primarily associated with their active support of the fascist authorities in Croatia in the 1940s. German sensitivity on this issue therefore led many to assume that the Germans would take a muted position on the issue of Croatian and Slovenian demands for recognition. But just the opposite was the case. The Germans advocated recognition of Croatia and Slovenia for both pragmatic and ideological reasons. Pragmatically, they argued, such recognition was the quickest and most effective way to bring peace and conciliation to the region. Ideologically, they claimed, such a policy would be consistent with the primacy the Germans have placed on the principle of self-determination. As one newspaper reported,

> The German case for recognition is more emotional than rational. The Germans are relatively near the fighting. To them, the struggle is of a Catholic people seeking the same self-determination that bought Germany together, faced with brutal subjugation by an expansionist, Communist Serbian regime. Some 400,000 Croats live and work in Germany, and hundreds of thousands of Germans have spent their summer holidays on Croatian beaches. Finally, there are bonds of history between Croatia and the German-speaking world, not least and to no one's credit during the Second World War.[36]

Germany's stridency was reflected in the fact that it was largely willing to ignore the protocol established in Brussels, and had 'invested the recognition debate with unequalled passion and single-mindedness'.[37] The product of this German pressure was a rushed decision by the EC states to support what many believed to be a premature recognition of the new states rather than provide sceptics with a substantial, initial example of the incapacity of EC members to formulate a common foreign policy. While Helmut Kohl, the German Chancellor, suggested that 'this was a great victory for German foreign policy', other vocal (mainly British) critics accused the Germans of employing bullying tactics, with one British Member of Parliament likening the German-induced recognition of the breakaway republics to 'throwing petrol on a bonfire'.[38] Yet the key point for our purpose is to emphasize that the result was compliance with German demands. The Germans engineered the agenda and got what they wanted through persuasion and influence rather than coercion, demonstrating their central role in influencing both the agenda and policies in the new European context.

Finally, we could point to the process that preceded German unification itself for recent evidence that the Germans have largely come to determine the agenda of deliberation. After all, the Germans got exactly what they wanted (in the form of unconditional unification) with remarkable speed. Yet discussions about Germany's role in NATO and the WEU often obscures German influence in a series of less publicized European, non-economic institutions where German influence has been present, such as in TREVI (Terrorism, Radicalism, Extremism, Violence, International), Europe's key intergovernmental system of co-operation in dealing with anti-terrorism policies which, Peter Katzenstein notes, was instituted in 1975 as a result of a German initiative, where the Germans have taken a leading role, and whose policies have largely responded to German concerns.[39]

CONCLUSION

The issue of the new Germany's role in a new Europe and a new world has already generated much academic debate in both Europe and the USA. The majority view sees Germany's unity as a boon to European unification and global peace. The minority view worries that a strong Germany will repeat the mistakes of the past. While the former points to *Modell Deutschland's* exemplary democracy and economy, the latter argues that the institutions have never been tested in a real crisis. The majority view better reflects our claims, although we differ with it on the issue of the effect on German power. Rather than presuming that German democracy and economy will serve to prevent a future hegemonic role for Germany in European affairs, we believe that such a role is guaranteed by precisely these factors – that Germany will take its place as a great power beside the United States and Japan. Successful democracies are powerful because of the consensual nature of their politics and the efficiency of their markets. The adage that Deutschmarks might go further than Panzers in extending German power seems quite compelling. German hegemony will not be the result of power politics but of its recognized economic and political position in both western and eastern Europe. The result will be a dominance by mutual consent rather than by external force.

Traditional assumptions about the intent of German elites in the context of a new, novel stage of the 'German question' therefore requires some reassessment. In the debate between the optimists and the pessimists concerning the contours of Germany's influence in Europe, it would appear that the latters' fears, though justified, are misplaced. German power will expand inadvertently rather than wilfully, economically and politically rather than militarily. National aggrandizement is not part of the German agenda but will be a necessary by-product of Germany's hegemonic position in Europe.[40] Rather than being plagued by the traditional characterizations of Germany's

Sonderweg and *Zwischenkultur*, authoritarianism and national chauvinism, the 'German question' today should be approached differently because it is one which belongs to the peaceful interaction of liberal democracies. None of Germany's neighbours and neither of the old superpowers worry any more about Germany's control of Europe through force of arms. While we have no doubt that German elites are driven by considerations of their own and Germany's interests, we suggest that the primary determinant of the contours of German power in Europe is more influenced by the attitudes of Germany's neighbours to the east and west.

It is not exclusively the structural centrality of the German economy that is likely to influence these neighbours in the policies they adopt. Ideas about how they are likely to succeed are just as influential. Tying themselves to the German economy through a collaborative monetary policy, purchasing German goods, involving themselves in joint ventures or learning the German language for trading purposes are just some examples of the spread of German influence.[41] But Hungarian adoption of German electoral laws and Czech attempts to model their business associations and trade unions along German lines (both in consultation with the representatives of the German government, and German labour and capital, respectively) are also less tangible examples of the spread of German influence.

Certainly a series of European institutions were initially designed with the intention of constraining German expansion. Both these efforts have failed in many cases – most pointedly the EC – and Germany is now the central pillar around which they turn. Yet it would be a mistake to infer that the pessimists' fears that Germany's elites are about to endorse a policy of territorial expansion will be realized. On the contrary, while Germany's political and economic elites consider themselves to be cosmopolitan internationalists, they paradoxically prefer a more limited role than that normally accorded to a great power. In fact, one might critically suggest that the ever-present wish on the part of many German liberals and leftists to see the Federal Republic merely as a larger Switzerland or Austria bespeaks either an incredible *naïveté* or a cynicism bordering on the irresponsible.[42]

The belief in the centrality of Germany's involvement – and indeed Germany's prosperity – to the development of Europe's other states therefore provides the Germans, *de facto*, with tremendous influence regardless of whether they want it or not. The borderline between simple influence and hegemony is (at least potentially) crossed when one couples the authority and credibility which the Germans possess by virtue of *Modell Deutschland* to the regional size and scope of their economy relative to those of the rest of Europe. A well-respected model is just that when it has a small and/or insulated economy. Conversely, it is a hegemon when it has a large, competitive, export-based economy. Germany has largely been admired and, assimilation being the sincerest form of flattery, has been considered a model of development, easily defeating its only serious challenger, the French model.

The Germans will therefore dominate the future of Europe. They will be its primary economic beneficiaries and most influential political actors. But this hegemony will be the product of mutual consent rather than coercion on the part of Germany's neighbours. Rather than emanating from German force, this new hegemony will result from the interactive effect of structure and ideas in an evolving Europe.

NOTES

1. The classic books in this genre include Ernst Haas. *The Uniting of Europe: Political, Social and Economic Forces, 1950–1957* (Stanford University Press, 1958); and Leon Lindberg and Stuart A. Scheingold, *Europe's Would-Be Polity: Patterns of Change in the European Community* (Englewood Cliffs: Prentice Hall, 1970).
2. Robert Gilpin, *U.S. Power and the Multinational Corporation* (New York: Basic Books, 1975), p.107.
3. Wolfram Hanrieder, *Germany, America, Europe: Forty Years of German Foreign Policy* (New Haven: Yale University Press, 1989), pp.5–7.
4. For a general discussion of the implications of assuming that states are interested in absolute rather than relative gains, see Joseph Grieco, *Co-operation Among Nations* (Ithaca: Cornell, 1990), p.10.
5. See Helmut Kohl, 'The Voice of Harmony that Stills National Rivalry', *Financial Times* Survey, *Financial Times* 29 October 1990, p.II.
6. Peter J. Katzenstein, *Policy and Politics in West Germany: The Growth of a Semi-Sovereign State* (Philadelphia: Temple, 1987).
7. See, for example, Josef Joffe's article 'Reunification II: This Time, No Hobnail Boots', *New York Times*, 30 September 1990, p.E3.
8. See Alexander Gerschenkron, *Bread and Democracy in Germany* (Ithaca: Cornell, 1989).
9. For two exceptions, see Ralf Dahrendorf, *Society and Democracy in Germany* (New York: Norton, 1979) and Simon Reich, *The Fruits of Fascism* (Ithaca: Cornell, 1990).
10. Cited in 'The Bridge-Building President', *Financial Times* Survey, *Financial Times*, 29 October 1990, p.III.
11. Franz Neumann, *Behemoth* (New York: Octagon, 1963).
12. Interview with Frederick Kempe, on C-Span, 21 December 1990.
13. The originator of this approach was Eckhart Kehr, whose contribution is analysed by Richard J. Evans in 'Introduction: Wilhelm II's Germany and the Historians', in Richard J. Evans (ed.), *Society and Politics in Wilhelmine Germany* (New York: Barnes & Noble, 1978), p.13. Other notable proponents of such radical interpretations include Fritz Fischer, *Germany's Aims in the First World War* (New York: Norton, 1967) and *The War of Illusions* (New York: Norton, 1975); John A. Moses, *The Politics of Illusion: The Fischer Controversy in German Historiography* (New York: Barnes & Noble, 1975); and Hans-Ulrich Wehler, *The German Empire 1871–1918* (Dover, NH: Berg Publishers, 1985).
14. For a brief summary of this debate, see Charles Maier, *The Unmasterable Past: History*

Holocaust, and the German National Identity (Cambridge, MA: Harvard University Press, 1988), pp.1–2. For a summary of this conservative intellectual tradition and the debates it engendered, see Reich, op. cit., pp.6–19.

15. As an example of German economic imperialism designed to address its raw materials policy, see Albert Hirschman, National Power and the Structure of Foreign Trade (Berkeley: University of California Press, 1969) on Nazi German treatment of the Balkan states in the 1930s; as applied to labour, see Edward Homze, Foreign Labor in Nazi Germany (Princeton: Princeton University Press, 1967); and for a more general argument suggesting that German militarism was a product of disjointed social structure, see note 8.

16. The original attitude of the participants of the Chequers conference was expressed in 'Be Nice to the Germans', in New York Times, 20 July 1990; for a critique of the 'Chequers' view on the Germans, see David Childs and Robert Gerald Livingston, 'Germany: a Joint Statement' in Politics and Society in Germany, Austria and Switzerland, Vol.3, No.1, Autumn 1990.

17. The initial, and most famous proponent of this view is Fritz Fischer, (see note 13); Hans-Ulrich Wehler (note 13) makes a similar argument.

18. Reported in The Independent, 19 December 1991.

19. This issue is discussed by Richard Gott in an article entitled 'State of Anxiety', Manchester Guardian Weekly, 7 October 1990.

20. Hermann Kantorowicz', The Spirit of British Policy and the Myth of the Encirclement of Germany, (Cambridge: Cambridge University Press, 1931).

21. 'Kohl pledges Global Role for Germany', Manchester Guardian Weekly, 7 October 1990.

22. Ibid.

23. For a discussion of the benign and malign versions of hegemonic stability theory, see Duncan Snidal, 'The Limits of Hegemonic Stability Theory', International Organization, Autumn 1985, pp.579–614. The most comprehensive statement of the realist position is provided by Stephen Krasner, 'State Power and the Structure of International Trade', World Politics, April 1976, pp.317–47.

24. Antonio Gramsci, Selections from the Prison Notebooks, ed. Q. Hoare and G. Nowell Smith (New York: International Publishers, 1971); Selections from Political Writings 1910–1920, ed. Q. Hoare (New York: International Publishers, 1977); and Selections from Political Writings, 1921–1926, ed. Q. Hoare (New York: International Publishers, 1978).

25. Gwyn A. Williams, 'The Concept of "Egemonia" in the Thought of Antonio Gramsci: Some Notes on Interpretation', Journal of the History of Ideas, Vol.21, October-December, 1960, p.591; and Joseph V. Femia, Gramsci's Political Thought: Hegemony, Consciousness, and the Revolutionary Process (Oxford: Clarendon Press, 1981), pp.35–50.

26. For a discussion of the importance of cultural hegemony to international relations see Bruce Russett, 'The Mysterious Case of the Vanishing Hegemon: or, Is Mark Twain Really Dead?', International Organization, Vol.39, No.2, Spring 1985, pp.228–30.

27. More broadly on this point, see Paul Piccone and G.L. Ulmen, 'Schmitt's "Testament" and the Future of Europe', Telos, No.83, Spring 1990, p.10.

28. See Andrei S. Markovits and Simon Reich. 'The New Face of Germany: Gramsci, Neorealism and Hegemony', Center for Europen Studies, Harvard University, Working Paper Series; and 'Modell Deutschland and the New Europe', Telos, No.89 (Fall 1991).

29. See, for example, 'British Bend on Single Currency but Resist Full European Unity' New York Times, 14 November 1991.

30. Paul J.J. Welfens, 'Creating a European Central Bank after 1992: Issues of EC Monetary Integration and Problems of Institutional Innovation', in Paul J.J. Welfens (ed.), European Monetary Integration: From German Dominance to an EC Central Bank (Berlin: Springer Verlag, 1991), p.15.

31. Ibid., p.6.

32. Ibid. See p.12 and especially p.15.

33. Ibid., p.9.

34. This view was expressed by David Wightman in a discussion with one of the authors.
35. See 'Economic Warfare, 1991 Style' and 'The Bundesbank's One-Two Punch', both in the *New York Times*, 22 December 1991.
36. 'An Unduly Negative Reaction', *The Independent*, 19 December 1991.
37. 'Germany Flexes its Muscles on Croatia's Behalf', *The Independent*, 19 December 1991.
38. See 'Kohl Hijacks Brussels Policy', *The Times*, 18 December 1991, and 'Hurd Raises Spectre of Past Wars over Balkan Rivalries', *The Independent*, 19 December 1991.
39. See Peter Katzenstein, 'Coping with Terrorism: Norms and Internal Security in Germany and Japan', paper delivered at the 1991 Annual Meeting of the American Political Science Association, p.14.
40. Thus, even though today's Germany might very well be 'peaceful, fearful, green', and 'favouring a low profile in world affairs', the objective fact is that Germany is in the process of becoming a hegemonic power in Europe and – quite likely – beyond. See 'Today's Germans: Peaceable, Fearful – and Green', and 'Germans Favour a Low Profile in World Affairs', *Financial Times*, 4 January 1991.
41. For details, see Markovits and Reich, 'The New Face of Germany'.
42. For some a general discussion and some interesting statistical data on the increasingly pacifistic and neutralist tendencies of both German masses and elites over the course of the last three decades, see Thomas Risse-Kappen. 'Public Opinion, Domestic Structure, and Foreign Policy in Liberal Democracies', *World Politics*, Vol.43, July 1991, pp.479–512.

German Security Policy after the Cold War: The Strategy of a Civilian Power in an Uncivil World

JAMES SPERLING

The collapse of the postwar security order created a security vacuum in Europe. The system of two opposing alliances buttressed by ideological enmity and dominated by two superpowers has been replaced by a reconfigured NATO that lacks a distinct and not easily defined military and political purpose, eastern European states that are adrift diplomatically and are struggling with the twin challenges of democracy and the market economy, and the disunion and fragmentation of the former Soviet Union. Germany, the key continental European partner of the United States in NATO, now faces a choice in the procurement of its security: whereas NATO had the character of an automatic alliance over the course of the postwar period – the Germans had little choice but to support NATO in exchange for an extended American deterrent – the collapse of the Warsaw Pact and the absence of a countervailing order in the eastern part of the European continent has had the unsettling effect of providing Germany with choice.[1] Although NATO still remains the essential institutional guarantor of security and stability in Europe and for Germany, it faces a longer-term challenge from the Conference on Security and Co-operation in Europe (CSCE), the European Community (EC), and the Western European Union (WEU).

The turbulence of Alliance relations and the uncertainties of the East–West conflict between 1949 and 1989 now appear, in retrospect, to be a long period of continuity, certainty, and stability. The content and direction of German security policy was narrowly circumscribed by the Federal Republic's membership of NATO and dependence upon the United States, and defined by the need to contain Soviet power in Europe. But the changes that have taken place in the European state system, particularly the unseemly and hasty disintegration of the former Soviet Union, and the prospect of an unwelcomed American retreat, driven by frustration with European demands exacerbated by severe domestic disabilities, raise a number of important questions about German security policy in the post-postwar world: how does Germany define its security interests in this world? What are the elements of continuity and change in German security policy? What institutions and institutional configuration do the Germans favour for the construction of a European security order? What are the implications of the changed international environment for the future of the German-American relationship? The German response to these questions frames the security debate in Europe and bears directly upon the prospects for the stability of the future European security order.

THE REDEFINITION OF GERMAN SECURITY

The German definition of security is no longer restricted to the traditional concern of guarding national borders from military invasion. Although the Germans retain a concern for protecting their territorial integrity, the immediacy of that concern has faded into the background. With the collapse of the Warsaw Pact and the disintegration of the Soviet Union, the question has since arisen: from whom and for what reason should the Germans prepare themselves militarily?

The Germans have refined and broadened their concept of security to conform with the pressures generated by, and to exploit the opportunities offered by, the evolution of the European state system. Today, German security is threatened not by an invasion of the Soviet army but by ethnic implosions in eastern, central, and southern Europe and the former Soviet Union that could draw the Germans into civil wars as mediators or as protectors of a threatened German minority; by the inability of Germany to control its borders in the event of mass migrations from eastern and southern Europe driven by political chaos (particularly in the former Soviet Union) or economic deprivation; by the proliferation of terrorist groups operating in Germany and reflecting indigenous political extremism as well as foreign political and religious extremism; and by threats to German economic security, defined not only in the traditional terms of access to markets and to raw materials, but in terms of protecting the German social market economy, the German preference for price stability and fiscal rectitude, and the German environment.

This broadening and redefinition of German security interests reflect a redefinition of the German state; the Germans have seized upon the idea that Germany must play the role of 'civilian' power in Europe; the role of a great or middle power defined militarily has been proscribed by history, conscience, treaty, and self-interest.[2] The German role in the future European order, although militarily circumscribed, is expansively defined economically, technologically, and politically. Germany desires full participation in the political and economic reconstruction of eastern Europe, in the creation of European political and economic union, in the restoration of the European environment, and in the construction of a functioning security structure encompassing the whole of Europe and based on the twin principles of democracy and the market economy. The Germans are unwilling (and unable) to contribute to the military requirements of global stability; it is recognized that these tasks are best left to the United States, France, and the United Kingdom. Germany remains satisfied to contribute to the economic requirements of security and to accelerate the demilitarization of interstate relations, particularly in Europe – a development that plays to Germany's economic capacity and not coincidentally enhances German influence in the reconstruction and recasting of the European order.

GERMAN SECURITY POLICY AND THE EVOLUTION
OF THE EUROPEAN STATE SYSTEM, 1949–92

In the postwar period, German foreign policy was framed and constrained by the American policy of double containment: the containment of the Soviet Union and the containment of Germany.[3] The containment of Germany gained its legitimacy for both the Germans and other Europeans (western and eastern) from the series of German-initiated wars beginning in 1871 and ending in 1945; and the containment of the Soviet Union gained its legitimacy from the bipolar structure of power that emerged at the end of the Second World War. The American policy was aided and abetted by what can be called Germany's self-conscious policy of self-containment,[4] a policy that began with the creation of the Federal Republic in 1949 when the Germans agreed to the Allies' reserving special rights in the Federal Republic, was promised by the *Grundgesetz* (the fledgling Federal Republic dedicated itself to the political unification of Europe), and was concretized with the German transferral of sovereignty to various multilateral and supranational institutions (e.g., the miscarried European Defence Community, NATO, the European Coal and Steel Community, and the European Economic Community). The process and practice of transferring sovereignty to such institutions was not limited to the Germans amongst the nations of the West, but, unlike those, the Germans felt compelled in the early part of their postwar history to prevent the spectre of a revanchist or revisionist Germany from arising and further complicating and debilitating German foreign policy, particularly with respect to the objective of unification. Consequently, the Germans conflated their national interests with the stated objectives of the security and economic institutions of the European and the Atlantic community; German policy makers have systematically translated German interests into the interests of the many over the course of the postwar period. For example, West Germans defined their economic interests in the language of European integration and the European Community; German political interests were framed in the language of a pan-European security order and the political unification of Europe (and Germany); and German security interests were expressed in terms reflecting the declaratory policies of NATO, particularly the Harmel Doctrine. This pattern continues today, albeit there has been a remarkable shift in German self-confidence and sense of importance.

The collapse of the postwar order has created an ambiguous and confounding international system. The Germans (and everyone else) are faced with an acknowledged and well-known but potentially introspective superpower (the United States), a politically fragmented and crippled military superpower (the Commonwealth of Independent States [CIS]), and, within the Atlantic context, two poles of economic power (the United States and a European Community anchored by Germany) that hover in equal measure around the pole of discord and the pole of collaboration. The dissolution of the Warsaw Pact–CMEA system underpinning Soviet power in Europe has left the United States without an adversary and Germany without a credible military or political threat to its territory or polity. As a consequence of these developments, the American policy of double containment has become irrelevant and inappropriate. It is irrelevant because the first object of American containment, the expansion of Soviet power into western Europe, no longer presents a credible security risk to the United States or its European allies. It is inappropriate because the American strategy for the 'new world order' relies heavily upon the successful drafting of Germany as a partner in leadership. Thus the American interests lay in effecting the positive objective of integrating Germany into the post-postwar order and preparing Germany to assume the responsibilities of a major power, rather than the negative objective of containing Germany and preventing the exercise of its power.

The Kohl–Genscher government has greeted and embraced the Bush administration's stated preference for Germany and America to act as partners in leadership in the Atlantic Alliance.[5] But the American strategy of creating a durable political axis linking Bonn and Washington has been tested and strained by several developments in the last two years: the Stavropol agreement between Chancellor Kohl and former President Gorbachev, without prior consultation with the United States, to limit the *Bundeswehr* to 370,000 men and to exclude NATO troops from the territory of the former German Democratic Republic (GDR); Germany's role as *Zahlmeister* (paymaster) during the Gulf War which transformed Britons and Americans into latter-day *condottiere*; the German–American disagreement over the level of financial aid to extend to the Soviet Union in early 1991, and the associated dispute over President Gorbachev's attendance at the Group of Seven (G-7) summit in July 1991; and a divergence of interest and response to developments in central and eastern Europe, most notably Germany's decision to recognize diplomatically the independent status of Slovenia and Croatia, despite the severe reservations of the other major western European powers and the active opposition of the United States.

The unravelling of the Soviet empire in eastern Europe and of the Soviet Union itself requires, from the German perspective, the integration of the former members of the Warsaw Pact, particularly Hungary, the Czech and Slovak Republic, and Poland – nations sharing a common border with a unified Germany – into the Western political, economic, and security systems. The political objectives of German foreign policy have not been fundamentally changed by the transformation of the European security order; Germany's foreign policy objectives remain the political and economic unification of Europe and the creation of a pan-European security system that preserves the indivisibility of German and American security.[6] Nor has the method of achieving those objectives changed: the Germans continue to prefer to work within multilateral and (increasingly) supranational or (con)federal frameworks. What has changed, however, is the content of those objectives, the actors involved, and the relative power position of the unified Germany in the process.

The German security strategy in the evolving European state system is a strategy of integration rather than independence, for exactly the same reasons as those offered by Adenauer and those in power since his time: it is a German responsibility to ensure that 'power politics' are never again the source of a European war; in the absence of integrative and confederal institutions constraining and managing German power, Germany's neighbours would be unsettled by German power and suspect its exercise; and only a pan-European solution combined with an integrative framework will secure the peace by laying to rest 'the German Problem' once and for all. Unstated reasons for preferring integrative institutions include the real leverage gained by the Germans over their partner-states in such settings: the Germans can make arguments framed in the pacific and non-threatening language of European economic prosperity or of European security rather than in the ominous and tainted language of German economic or security interests. German history and the acute awareness of that history by Germans and Germany's neighbours will ensure that Germany continues to tread the path followed for over 40 years – as Theo Sommer has noted, 'normality' in German foreign policy must be defined differently from British, French or

American foreign policy in terms of content, conception, and execution.[7] An important non-military component of the German security strategy is the deepening and widening of the European Community: the Germans hope to contain the economic and political disintegration of eastern Europe by providing a home port for the nations of north-central Europe and a stabilizing magnet for the CIS. Embedding Germany in the European Community will also reassure Germany's neighbours of German intentions and place limitations on Germany's freedom of action, two outcomes that lower the risk of co-operation with and of coercion by Germany. But this dependence upon the EC is contingent upon the continued viability of NATO and the American connection. The American connection reinsures the Germans against untoward events in eastern Europe that the EC or a 'civilian' power is presently ill-equipped to deal – for example, mediating a civil war or stabilizing a disintegrating neighbour state – and reassures Germany's neighbours that the United States is available to countervail the German exercise of power, a reassurance that, paradoxically, allows the Germans to press forward with a foreign policy agenda tailored to German interests and preferences in Europe.

The post-postwar German security strategy, expressed as it is in the idiom of European political and economic union, depends upon the continued demilitarization of the European state system. The demilitarization of international relations – what Foreign Minister Genscher has called the helvetiaization of politics in Europe – reduces American leverage over the Germans on monetary and trade issues, because it devalues the American extended nuclear deterrent, the source of American influence in Europe and leverage over the Germans; and it enhances German influence with the CIS, its European neighbours and the United States, because it plays to the source of German power, its economic capacity. But without European union, German foreign policy would not be free from the suspicion and fear of German hegemony or the unwelcomed imposition of German preferences on its weaker European neighbours. And if the progressive demilitarization of the European state system is slowed or reversed, Germany will face a comparative disadvantage in its dealings not only with the Americans, but with the French and the British: the Germans may find themselves once again trading economic concessions in exchange for an American (French or British) security guarantee of questionable value.

THE INSTITUTIONS OF EUROPEAN SECURITY: THE GERMAN PERSPECTIVE

The redefinition of German security and the changed (and changing)

European state system have shaped and reshaped the role and promise of the existing institutions of European security. The German envisioned role for NATO, the Conference on Security and Co-operation in Europe, the European Community, and the Western European Union are contingent upon the evolution of the European state system and the definition of German interests, both of which will be influenced by the path taken by the erstwhile republics of the former Soviet Union, and by the evolution of the relationship amongst the major European powers and between Europe and America.

NATO: From Military Alliance to Transatlantic Security Bridge?

NATO, and the extended American nuclear deterrent, guaranteed German security in the postwar period, supported the German effort to achieve western European political and economic integration, and was considered essential to the eventual unification of the two Germanies. Before unification, the German adherence to NATO derived from the structure of power in the international system and the geostrategic position of Germany in Europe. It was not surprising, therefore, to find Chancellor Kohl stating in 1988 that 'the Western Alliance is a part of our *Staatsraison*' or that NATO is 'the cornerstone of [German] security policy'.[8] The Germans reassured the Americans that they did not want to replace NATO with an autonomous European security structure; embraced the strategy of flexible response; rejected the option of a denuclearized Europe; and dismissed the possibility of a 'third zero' for land-based nuclear systems under 500 kilometres.[9]

The fundamental changes that transformed the European state system between 1988 and 1991 altered the German position on the prospect of the denuclearization of Europe and the viability of flexible response. By the summer of 1990, Defence Minister Stoltenberg began the slow reversal of German policy: although the Germans did not advocate the denuclearization of Europe, they greeted with enthusiasm the American decision neither to deploy a follow-on to the *Lance* short-range nuclear missile nor to modernize nuclear artillery. The German preference on nuclear matters was for a new form of singularization: the deployment of nuclear weapons at sea (or in the United Kingdom or France) would leave the Germans defended and relieve them of the political costs or military risks attending the stationing of nuclear weapons on German soil. Moreover, Stoltenberg advocated a lessened dependence upon nuclear deterrence in favour of a system that provided mutual security and stability to the European area.[10] In his policy declaration of January 1991, Chancellor Kohl urged the United States and the Soviet Union to begin negotiations to remove land-based, short-range nuclear weapons as well as nuclear artillery from Europe; and greeted as a timely response to the changed political status quo in Europe the NATO decision to refashion the concept of forward defence and to relegate nuclear weapons to weapons of 'last resort'. By February 1991, Foreign Minister Genscher stated unequivocally that a continuation of the disarmament process in Europe was essential and that 'the short-range nuclear weapons and nuclear artillery must disappear from Europe'.[11] The Alliance conformed with Genscher's exhortation by the time of the Rome NATO summit, in November 1991, when the allies agreed to reduce the number of sub-strategic nuclear weapons by 80 per cent.[12] But the Rome Declaration only ratified President Bush's decision in late September 1991 to eliminate all American land-and-sea-based, short-range nuclear weapons, including nuclear artillery, stationed in Europe, retaining only 'an effective air-delivered capability in Europe', a capability viewed as 'essential to NATO's security'.[13]

The German–American security tie within NATO has been and remains essential for German security and European stability. But the sources of cohesion in the Alliance have undergone a subtle, but significant change: NATO member states, to be sure, share common security interests, but the Germans argue that the glue that holds the Alliance together is the values common to them.[14] For the Germans, the American role in Europe has evolved into the explicit role of nightwatchman: the American role and responsibility 'in and for Europe [remains] of critical meaning for the peace and security of our continent and above all for the unified Germany in the middle of that continent'.[15] The necessity of NATO for the success of the EC or the CSCE in the security field has forced the Germans to argue against the proposition that NATO, the EC, and the CSCE have conflicting purposes or conflicting logics; hence the slogan '*sowohl-als-auch*' (this as well as that) and the emphatic rejection of '*entweder-oder*' (either this or that).[16] The Germans desire to have it three ways – NATO and the American security guarantee, the European Community and a single European security identity, and the CSCE and a pan-European security order. But this position has not left them shy about giving pride of place to NATO and accentuating the continuing need for an American troop presence in Europe.[17]

NATO remains attractive to the Germans because it provides them with a number of external economies: first, the stability afforded by the Alliance 'reach[es] beyond the immediate circle of its member states' and contributes to the stability of the reforming nations of eastern and central Europe;[18] second, NATO serves as a hedge against neo-isolationism in the United States;[19] and finally, as Defence Minister Stoltenberg noted,

NATO is 'the single functioning security structure in Europe' and serves as a yardstick against 'fair-weather security structures' that are the pretenders to NATO's role.[20] Within the German government there is general agreement that NATO, as the sole functioning security structure in Europe, is necessary for the foreseeable future. It is also clear that the Germans believe that, without NATO, the CSCE and probably European political union would be non-starters.[21] This position answers in the affirmative the question: is NATO a key element of the German security strategy? But it also raises a number of other significant questions: is NATO important simply because it is the only realistic alternative facing the Germans? Is NATO important because it remains part and parcel of a unified Germany's *Staatsraison*? Is NATO important because it is the foundation upon which a collective security system from the Atlantic to the Urals can be safely constructed? Or has NATO merely become, in the words of of Foreign Minister Genscher, 'a transatlantic security bridge for the whole of Europe, for the democracies of eastern and western Europe'.[22] The answers to these questions turn upon the expectations that the Germans have for the CSCE, the EC, and the WEU in the future European security order.

CSCE: The Security Institution of the Future?

The CSCE will serve two specific functions for the Germans in the future European order: it promises the institutionalization of a pan-European peace order based upon the principle of collective security; and it offers an additional mechanism for overcoming the 'prosperity barrier' (*Wohlstandsgrenze*) between the nations of western and eastern Europe with the establishment of a free market regime throughout Europe.

The Germans agree with former President Gorbachev that the security concerns of Germany's neighbours can be resolved only in a 'common European house', although the intellectual lineage of 'a common European house' is traced not to President Gorbachev but to Chancellor Adenauer and the former Finance and Defence Minister Franz-Josef Strauss.[23] Despite the Germanic pedigree of the CSCE, the German government's attitude towards the CSCE remains somewhat ambivalent. In repeated policy statements, Chancellor Kohl first expresses German dependence upon NATO for German security, then discusses the prospects for a European security identity that would serve as the second pillar of the Atlantic security system, and only then mentions the CSCE, normally highlighting the institution's future promise as the framework for a pan-European peace order. But even then, Chancellor Kohl (and Foreign Minister Genscher) carefully note that any European security arrangement dominated by the CSCE cannot exclude the two North

American powers.[24] Nonetheless, the CSCE frames Germany's security (and economic) aspirations in eastern and central Europe.[25]

At this stage of the evolution of the European state system, the Kohl–Genscher government views the CSCE process as supplementary to NATO in the following sense: NATO provides insurance against any military threat to the territorial integrity of Germany, while the CSCE makes a positive contribution to European security by integrating the former Warsaw Pact member states, including the CIS into the western economic and political orbit. Yet the Germans remain dependent upon the United States: the success of the CSCE requires a continuing American imprimatur to lend it legitimacy and effectiveness.[26]

The Germans argue that economic envy (*Wirtschaftsneid*) on the part of other nations in Europe, rather than the exercise or exploitation of Germany's economic power (*Wirtschaftsmacht*), is an important and very real threat to the stability of Europe, and consequently to the German polity and economy.[27] Although the EC plays the dominant role in securing the economic dimension of German security, the CSCE provides an important mechanism for constructing a stable and prosperous European economic space. The Germans proposed and hosted the 1990 CSCE Bonn Conference on economic co-operation in Europe. The Bonn CSCE document obligated the non-market economies of Europe to institute price reform, to implement policies that would lead to currency convertibility, and to adopt the principles of the market economy. The Germans believe that the Bonn CSCE document on economic co-operation provides a stable framework for the creation of a single, integrated European economic space reaching from the Atlantic to the Urals; that, in effect, it establishes a European economic regime favouring the principles of the market economy.[28] The emphasis on the economic aspect of the relations amongst the nations of Europe reflects the German redefinition of security, and it has the practical consequence of altering the calculus of power in the European area: it shifts attention away from the military potential of a state to its productive capability and rate of technological innovation, a development that would further strength German diplomacy at the expense of France and Britain. Moreover, the German government views pan-European economic co-operation as an essential aspect of the CSCE process because the basis for social stability, and therefore for national security, is economic welfare.[29] For the Germans, security co-operation is contingent upon economic co-operation,[30] an assumption that goes a long way to explain German enthusiasm for European economic and monetary union as well as the Bonn CSCE document.

The CSCE plays an important function for the Germans that NATO cannot and the EC is unlikely to play, now or in the future: CSCE provides an institutional mechanism for integrating the republics of the CIS into a pan-European security and economic space without necessarily compromising or threatening the geopolitical and military logic of NATO or undermining the progress towards European political union within the framework of the EC. The meaning and importance of the CSCE for the Germans may be located as well in Foreign Minister Genscher's assertion that 'the German–Soviet relationship possesses a central importance for the stability of Europe'.[31] The fragmentation of the Soviet Union and the uncertain future of the CIS make it unclear whether Germany will have a lone partner or a number of partners in the place of the Soviet Union. But if the CIS survives (or is replaced by a loose confederation of states conducting a common foreign policy), then only the CSCE provides a mechanism for ordering that relationship within a multilateral framework. The CSCE unburdens Russo–German co-operation by diminishing the spectre of a second Rapallo, because the relationship between a Russian-dominated CIS and Germany will be conducted within a multilateral framework.

The European Community: Second Pillar or Independent Power?

The political unification of Europe, a foreign policy objective mandated by the *Grundgesetz*, was intended initially as a method of burying European animosities built up after seven decades of intermittent war, and as a method of eradicating its source, Franco–German competition for European hegemony. For the Germans it also served the larger purpose of reintegrating Germany into the society of western states after the Second World War; and it eventually became the idiom in which German interests, particularly in the economic sphere, were expressed and identified. The combination of historical escape and tactical realism has left the legacy of a genuine German dedication to European political and economic integration, albeit on German terms.

Today leading German politicians describe the European Community as 'the sheet anchor of Europe', as 'the stable anchor in a stormy sea', and as 'the cornerstone of European stability and an essential component of the future European political structure'.[32] The Germans claim that, since the EC is the only 'area of stability' (*Stabilitätsraum*) in Europe, it demonstrates that stability on the European continent need not reflect nor depend upon military power. Rather, stability in the EC reflects a unique combination of culture, technology, a functioning social market economy, and the observance of human rights;[33] thus the EC is a model for the rest of Europe and an essential part of the future European security order. The EC plays a triple role in the German security strategy for Europe: first, the progress towards political union and economic and monetary union provides a magnet for the reforming states of central and eastern Europe that will contribute to the erasure of the 'Wohlstandsgrenze' between capitalist and protocapitalist Europe;[34] second, the inevitable trend towards the creation of a common security and foreign policy will enable 'Europe' to function as a second pillar within NATO and assume responsibilities commensurate with Europe's economic and military power;[35] and third, the political unification of Europe will create the framework for common immigration, asylum, and anti-terrorism laws that will protect the German domestic order.[36] Moreover, the European Community (along with NATO and CSCE) assures Germany's neighbours and partners that Germany is cognizant of and will respect the 'security needs and the feelings of all Europeans, understandably and above all our neighbours'; and German enthusiasm for the EC demonstrates, at least from the German perspective, that Germany has renounced, once and for all, the 'national unilateralism and the Sonderweg' that has shaped modern European history.[37]

In the discussions leading to the Maastricht summit in December 1991, particularly within the intergovernmental conference to draft the EC treaty on European political union, the Germans insisted that political union requires the co-ordination and convergence of the security and the foreign policies of the member states of the Community. Moreover, the Germans view the process of European political union and the absorption of the WEU by the EC as a major contribution to the stabilization of Europe and the creation of an effective second pillar in the Atlantic Alliance. The benefits of a European security identity flow from the 'enormous economic, social, and ecological problems facing the world' that NATO is ill-equipped to deal with.[38] Thus the German dependence upon NATO – as reinsurance against the unravelling of the reform process in eastern Europe and the CIS and as the nexus for the co-ordination of policy on a broad array of issues ranging from security, the environment, to debt relief – has not precluded a European option for Germany, an option seen as complementary to rather than competitive with continued German membership in NATO or partnership with the United States.[39]

The European Community also holds the key to a critical problem facing the Germans and western Europe at large, namely, the prospect of mass migrations from the pauperized nations of eastern Europe and the impoverished regions of the Third World, particularly the nations of the Balkans and Mediterranean basin.[40] The concurrent freeing of travel in eastern Europe and the collapse of those nations' economies have left open the possibility of mass migrations that pose 'a special risk factor to western Europe'.[41] It poses an especial risk to the Germans, given the present financial burden of reconstructing the eastern part of the country, the unpleasant fact that Germany is the preferred destination of economic refugees from eastern Europe for cultural as well as financial reasons,[42] and the liberal provisions of Articles 16 (which guarantees the right to political asylum) and 116 (which provides a citizenship guarantee to ethnic Germans living in eastern Europe). The large number of foreign residents in Germany, now accounting for almost eight per cent of the German population, and the economic dislocations associated with German unification have increased the attractiveness of the extreme right *Republikaner* party and the incidence of violence against non-Germans in both eastern and western Germany. The legacy of National Socialist Germany has made it virtually impossible for any of the mainstream political parties in Germany to advocate a national solution to the immigration problem by repealing or significantly amending Articles 16 and 116 of the constitution; the SPD and FDP are set against any change in the *Grundgesetz* and the CDU/CSU's hesitation is located in the uncertain external ramifications of such an action. The Kohl–Genscher government has adopted the position that there should be no immigration to Germany from nations outside the EC; and the justification for this policy is located in the traditional homogeneity of European nation-states.[43] But the Germans do desire a mechanism for stanching the flow of economic refugees that are placing a strain on the already strained German economy and polity. The Germans actively seek the cover of a common European immigration policy that will override the provisions of *Grundgesetz* and prevent economic refugees from finding a safe haven in the Federal Republic.

The fear of economic refugees and non-German immigrants is reinforced by two other concerns: the proliferation of terrorist groups in Germany and the continuation of eastern European civil wars on German soil. The *Verfassungsschutzbericht 1988*, for example, listed 101,000 foreigners involved in 112 extremist groups;[44] and Germany is now the home of Croatian extremists, some of whom have left Germany to fight against Serbia in the civil war and some of whom were arrested for smuggling weapons to Croatian forces.[45] The prospect that the Yugoslav civil war will be continued by terrorist means from or on German soil remains hypothetical, but the prospects for continued political turmoil in eastern and southern Europe remain good, as do the prospects of the conflicts being played out in the Federal Republic by the large number of recent immigrants and asylum seekers. The Germans recognize that the problem of asylum and mass migration cannot be solved within the national context and requires a solution at the community level; and the

Germans believe that the inability to control their national borders poses perhaps the most immediate and real threat to the stability of their economy and polity.[46]

Western European Union: Atlanticism Reaffirmed or Gaullism Re-established?

The relationship between the European Community and the Western European Union did not gain momentum until 1990, but the contemporary 'prehistory' of the WEU is instructive. When French Prime Minister Chirac suggested the revitalization of the WEU and the creation of a European security identity in December 1986, the European member states responded (in October 1987) with a 'Platform on European Security Interests'. This drew on the Atlanticist, Gaullist, and Europeanist catechisms. American and European security were indivisible and the Alliance required a credible European pillar. But, at the same time, the protection of European interests in the Atlantic area required the creation of a European security identity independent of the United States. Moreover, the Europeans agreed that 'the construction of an integrated Europe will remain incomplete as long as it does not include security and defence';[47] and the revitalization of the WEU was linked to the process of European political union.

Two ambiguities arose from the envisaged role of the WEU: first, would it become the second pillar of the Atlantic Alliance or the security and defence policy arm of the European Community? And, second, would it promise intensified security co-operation or conflict between the United States and Europe, not only on security issues that were 'out of area', but on security issues within the purview of NATO as well. In 1990, however, President Mitterrand and Chancellor Kohl agreed that both NATO and the WEU were essential for continued stability and co-operation in Europe; and that both institutions occupied the same 'security area' and needed to intensify their co-operation.[48] President Mitterrand and Chancellor Kohl later proposed that the intergovernmental conference of the EC concerning political union should consider how the WEU could be strengthened and how it could be merged with the European Community.[49] The purpose was twofold: it could serve as a transitional institution before the creation of federal Europe, and would thus enable the Europeans to jump-start their security co-operation by grafting an existing institution on to the EC; and it would enable France and Germany to co-operate on security policy without forcing France to choose between an ever-ephemeral (and pointless) security independence, and without forcing the Germans to make (an increasingly irrelevant) choice between the United States and France, and between NATO and Europe. The importance vested in the WEU reflects the German calculation that European political union has made the concept (and practice) of national military autonomy outmoded.[50] The Viaden communiqué of the WEU in June 1991 did not clarify the ultimate shape of the institutional linkages between the WEU, the EC, and NATO; in fact, the WEU ministers settled to have it both ways: the communiqué described the WEU as an important component of the process of European union; as the basis for expanding defence co-operation between the member states of the WEU and the EC; and as the institutional vehicle for strengthening the European pillar of the Atlantic Alliance.[51] This policy position was common to the communiqués issued by the European Council at the June 1991 Luxembourg meeting and by the NATO Council at the June 1991 Copenhagen meeting, and it was even included in the Franco–German–Polish Weimar declaration.[52]

The German policy position shifted firmly in favour of subordinating the WEU to the EC, beginning in July 1991, when Foreign Minister Genscher stated that the 'WEU must form part of European union in accordance with the Hague Platform of 1987'.[53] In October 1991 the institutional relationship between the WEU, NATO, and the EC became a highly charged affair when France and Germany responded to the Anglo–Italian proposal that the WEU should remain subordinated to NATO, represent Europe 'out of area' and exist independently of the EC. The Franco–German counter-proposal suggested that the WEU should serve as the basis of a European security identity within as well as outside Europe, and that it should be subordinate to the EC for security issues within Europe as well as 'out of area'. The Franco–German proposal called for closer institutional co-operation between the EC and the WEU at all levels, for closer co-ordination between WEU member states in order to reach common positions within NATO, for moving the WEU general secretariat from London to Brussels, and for expanding relations with the other nations of Europe in conformity with the Copenhagen and the Vianden communiqué.[54]

At the Maastricht summit, the Europeans agreed to the Franco–German position in substance, but employed language allowing the British to claim that the WEU will remain subordinate to NATO. The EC treaty on political union commits the member states to 'the eventual framing of a common defence policy, which might in time lead to a common defence . . .', and identified the WEU as an 'integral part of the development of the European union'. The treaty also provided that the WEU could be requested to 'elaborate and implement decisions and actions of the union which have defence implications'.[55] Although language in the treaty provided that the evolution of this relationship

between the WEU and the EC be compatible with NATO, it is also clear
that the Franco–German design for a separate security identity won the
day. What remains uncertain, however, is the future relationship of the
WEU and the EC to NATO, and that in turn raises the question about the
future relationship between Germany and the United States.

THE FUTURE EUROPEAN SECURITY ORDER:
THE GERMAN ARCHITECTURE

The Germans increasingly view NATO as a short- to medium-term
vehicle for addressing the symptoms of the security dilemma facing the
Europeans and Germans, and for reinsuring Germany against the failure
of the CSCE, the institution viewed as best suited to the task of resolving
the conflicting demands of Germany's security interests. The EC is
viewed by the Germans as the economic and political magnet for north-
central and Nordic Europe, as the 'sheet anchor' for all of Europe, as the
core of a future European (con)federation, and as the vehicle for ensuring
Germany's economic security. The Germans consider the WEU as the
most European security institution, because it will allow a uniting Europe
to forge a single foreign and defence policy without requiring the
Europeans to jettison NATO prematurely.[56] The fortunes of the WEU,
however, are dependent upon the process of European political
unification.

The institutional solution to Germany's security dilemma – retaining
the American extended deterrent, building an independent Europe, and
creating an inclusive pan-European security system – cannot be found in a
simple choice between NATO, CSCE, the EC, or WEU. The Germans,
in fact, reject the notion that a choice must be made. For the Germans, all
four security institutions are compatible and mutually reinforcing. Each
serves specific and interrelated tasks for the Germans. NATO reinsures
against the unravelling of the post-postwar order as the Germans (and
other Europeans) construct a (con)federal Europe and a European
security identity. The CSCE is inclusive (both the United States and the
states of the CIS are members), provides a framework for the continued
demilitarization of European foreign affairs with accelerated arms
control and disarmament, and furnishes Europe with embryonic regimes
that lend support to the embrace of the market economy and democracy
in eastern Europe and the CIS. And the EC and the WEU provide the
Germans with a mechanism for ensuring a German voice in the evolution
of the European order, for providing the Germans with the
consummation of the constitutionally dictated objective of European
unification, for creating a European security identity capable of

contesting American pretensions in Europe, and for constructing a political entity capable of withstanding pressures from a renascent Russia. Despite the seeming compatibility of these institutions, the logic of the German security strategy leads inexorably to the conclusion that the CSCE and the EC will inevitably become the preferred institutions of European security.

Yet paradoxically NATO remains the key institution in the German strategy: NATO is considered 'essential' in the creation of a European political and security identity; NATO is considered to be the only credible guarantor of European (and German) security; NATO serves as reinsurance against the misfiring of the political and economic liberalization in eastern Europe or the political disintegration of the former Soviet Union into any number of disparate Republics; and only NATO can support the transition to a CSCE-dominated pan-European security system by providing a stable international environment.

The Germans refuse to make an unambiguous choice between these institutions, partly because there is no compelling reason to do so at this juncture and partly because the institutions are, in fact, complementary rather than competitive, at least for now. The German preoccupation with the institutional character of the post-postwar order and the mutual dependence of these institutions reflect, no doubt, two lessons of history: first, peace and stability in Europe are only possible if Germany is closely tied to its neighbours in a manner that benefits each reciprocally; and, second, NATO, has provided Germany and the other European democracies with the longest period of peace in contemporary history.[57]

CONCLUSION: GERMANY, AMERICA, AND EUROPE

The Germans seek the creation of a European state system congenial to the instruments, concerns, and calculations of power and interest of a 'civilian power'. NATO, the instrument of American influence in Europe, is ill-equipped to cope with the real security threats facing the Federal Republic: economic collapse in eastern Europe and mass migrations to Germany. Consequently, German foreign policy has vested great importance in the success and expansion of the CSCE, the EC and more recently the WEU. The German security strategy has three elements: self-containment of German power in order that Germany may use its power to influence its European neighbours to effect German policy objectives; the creation of an independent Europe capable of withstanding American pressures on economic issues; and the continued demilitarization of Europe that depends upon the sustained growth of democracy and the free market in the former member states of the Warsaw Pact.

In the short term, there is no manifest conflict of interest between the United States and the Federal Republic on the institutional configuration of the present European security order. The United States favours the continuing dominance of NATO, and the continuing influence that NATO extends to the United States. Although the United States casts an increasingly wary and jaundiced eye on the ultimate purposes and implications of the European Community and the WEU, the success and strengthening of both are important if there is to be a second pillar of the Alliance. The CSCE is not central to the American security calculus; its importance has been diminished by the collapse of the Soviet empire. For the Germans, these institutions are interdependent and reinforcing; each services a different aspect of German security policy. NATO ensures Germany's military security and provides a fail-safe environment where Germany can pursue its economic and political objectives in Europe. The EC ensures Germany's economic security and welfare, provides an important mechanism whereby Germany can effectively wield its influence, and contributes to the development of a credible second pillar within NATO, as does the institutional elaboration of the WEU. The CSCE has established, particularly with the *Charter of Paris*, a political regime setting democracy as the political norm and an economic regime identifying capitalism as the economic norm. It is incontrovertible that German policy depends upon NATO as reinsurance against the failure of the others.

The institutional configurations and institutions favoured by the United States and the Federal Republic reveal an intractable and underlying source of discord in German–American relations. For the Germans, NATO is but an instrument for achieving the larger (and longer-term) objectives of pan-European security and economic co-operation, and provides the Germans with some insurance against unforeseen developments in eastern and southern Europe. The Americans are content to preserve NATO, draft Germany as their partner in leadership within the Alliance, and prolong American influence over German foreign policy. As the Germans grow more comfortable with the exercise of power, as the process of European union enables the Germans to exercise their power through and in the name of European institutions, and as eastern and western Europe grow closer together economically and politically, the time will come when NATO – and the American security connection – will have outlived their usefulness for the Federal Republic.

The prospects for a German–American partnership framed by NATO are contingent upon the political evolution of the former Soviet Union and the European state system. Instability and the fear of it in Europe, rather than the American nuclear deterrent, sustain German dependence upon the United States. The prospects for the German security strategy are contingent upon the evolution of the European state system. If this continues upon a trajectory of political union and demilitarization, the CSCE and the EC-WEU will provide the institutional framework for the security needs of a 'civilian power'. It remains to be seen, however, if the world remains an uncivil place.

NOTES

1. For an extended discussion of NATO as a 'fated community' (Schicksalsgemeinschaft), Emil J. Kirchner and James Sperling, 'The Future Germany and the Future of NATO', see *German Politics*, Vol.1, No.1 (April 1992).
2. See Theo Sommer, 'Die Deutschen an die Front?', *Die Zeit, #13*, 29 March 1991, p.3.
3. This theme is a dominant one in Wolfram F. Hanrieder, *Germany, America, Europe: Forty Years of German Foreign Policy* (New Haven: Yale, 1989).
4. See, for example, the comments of Bundesminister für besondere Aufgaben Rudolf Seiters, 'Perspektiven der Deutschlandpolitik im geeinten Europa', 30 November 1990, *Bulletin des Presse- und Informationsamtes* (hereafter *Bulletin*), Nr.141 (5 December 1990), p.1485.
5. For example, see the remarks of Chancellor Helmut Kohl, 'Tanner Lecture an der Universität Kalifornien in Berkeley'. 13 September 1991, Nr.102 (20 September 1991), p.811; and of Bundesminister des Auswärtigen Hans-Dietrich Genscher, 'Europäisch-japanische Zusammenarbeit im Aufbau einer neuen Welt', 13 September 1991, *Bulletin*, Nr.101 (19 September 1991), p.801.
6. Helmut Kohl, note 5, p.812.
7. See Sommer, note 2.
8. Helmut Kohl, 'Die Streitkräfte als wichtigstes Instrument der Sicherheitspolitik', 13 December 1988, in *Presse und Informationsamt der Bundesregierung, Bulletin*, Nr.175 (16 December 1988), pp.1550–1.
9. This rejection was qualified by the statement that the structure of the Alliance's nuclear weapon forces depended 'upon the changes in the political situation and the military threat, of the results of arms control and disarmament negotiations, and of technological developments'. Kohl, note 8, p.1552. See similar statements by Chancellor Kohl: 'Regierungerklärung des Bundeskanzlers vor dem Deutschen Bundestag. Arbeitsprogramm der Bundesregierung: Perspektiven für die neunziger Jahre'. 27 April 1989, *Bulletin*, Nr.40 (28 April 1989), p.370.
10. Bundesminister der Verteidigung Gerhard Stoltenberg, 'Künftige Perspektiven deutscher Sicherheitspolitik', 13 June 1990, *Bulletin*, Nr.76 (14 June 1990), p.654.
11. Compare these statements with those made by Chancellor Kohl in his 1989 Regierungserklärung, where he acknowledged the need for land-based short-range nuclear weapons and nuclear artillery to sustain the strategy of deterrence. Kohl, in fact, stated that there was 'no alternative to [nuclear] deterrence' to prevent the outbreak of war. Helmut Kohl, in note 9. Bundesminister des Auswärtigen Hans-Dietrich Genscher, 'Eine Vision für das ganze Europa'. 3 February 1991, *Bulletin*, Nr.14 (6 February 1991), p.92.
12. 'NATO-Gipfelkonferenz in Rom: Erklärung von Rom über Frieden und Zusammenarbeit', 8 November 1991, *Bulletin*, Nr.128 (13 November 1991), p.1034.
13. 'Remarks by President Bush on Reducing US and Soviet Nuclear Weapons', *New York Times*, 28 September 1991, p.A4. The American decision to eliminate ground-and sea-based tactical nuclear weapons from the European theatre was reciprocated by President Gorbachev in early October, *New York Times*, 6 October 1991, p.A1.

14. Chancellor Kohl, for example, stated that 'NATO must always be understood as a community of values . . . and this means that we neither can nor desire the replacement of NATO'. See his remarks in 'Die Rolle Deutschlands in Europa', 13 March 1991, *Bulletin*, Nr.33 (22 March 1991), p.244. See also Helmut Kohl, 'Aufgaben deutscher Politik in den neunziger Jahren', 20 May 1991, *Bulletin*, Nr.56 (22 May 1991), p.443.

15. Helmut Kohl, 'Regierungserklärung des Bundeskanzlers vor dem Deutschen Bundestag: Unsere Verantwortung für die Freiheit', 30 January 1991, *Bulletin*, Nr.11 (31 January 1991), pp.73–4.

16. See Helmut Kohl, 'Die Rolle Deutschlands in Europa', note 14, p.245, and 'Aufgaben deutscher Politik in den neunziger Jahren', note 14, p.441.

17. Helmut Kohl, 'Verantwortung für das Zusammenwachsen Deutschlands und Europas', 6 June 1991, *Bulletin*, Nr.64 (7 June 1991), p.513. See also Minister of Finance Theodor Waigel, 'Haushaltsgesetz vor dem Deutschen Bundestag', 3 September 1991, *Bulletin*, Nr.93 (4 September 1991), p.747. Waigel, in response to SPD criticism that he ignored the CSCE, argues that NATO and the CSCE are not in opposition to one another and that 'both are necessary instruments for peace in Europe and the world'.

18. Helmut Kohl, 'Erstes Treffen des Rates der Aussenminister der Teilnehmerstaaten der KSZE', 19 June 1991, *Bulletin*, Nr.72 (22 June 1991), p.579. This position reflected the outcome of the Copenhagen NATO Summit on 6 June 1991 where the allies made an effort to reassure the nations of the former Warsaw Pact with language that stopped short of offering a unilateral security guarantee (*New York Times*, 7 June 1991, p.A1).

19. Hans-Dietrich Genscher, note 11.

20. Gerhard Stoltenberg, 'Zukunftsaufgaben der Bundeswehr im vereinten Deutschland', 13 March 1991, *Bulletin*, Nr.29 (15 March 1991), p.215. See also Stoltenberg, 'Der Selbstverständnis des Soldaten in der Bundeswehr von morgen', 17 June 1991, *Bulletin*, Nr.70 (19 June 1991), p.566.

21. Gerhard Stoltenberg, 'Deutsche Einheir und europäische Sicherheit', 1 May 1990, *Bulletin*, Nr.52 (5 May 1990), p.406.

22. Hans-Dietrich Genscher, note 11.

23. On the attribution to Adenauer, see Gerhard Stoltenberg, 'Erklärung der Bundesregierung. Die Bundeswehr in den neunziger Jahren', 7 December 1989, *Bulletin*, Nr.140 (8 December 1989), p.1189 and 'Sicherheits Fragen eines kunftigen geeinten Deutschland', 19 February 1990, *Bulletin*, Nr.28 (21 February 1990), p.218.

24. See Helmut Kohl, note 15, pp.72–5, and in note 17. See also Hans-Dietrich Genscher, 'Rede des Bundesaussenministers vor den Vereinten Nationen', 25 September 1991, *Bulletin*, Nr.104 (26 September 1991), p.825.

25. The German–Polish Treaty of June 1991, for example, is littered with references to the various CSCE meetings and documents; and Article 3 of the Treaty commits the contracting parties to 'seek peace through the elaboration of co-operative structures of security for the whole of Europe . . . [including the full implementation of] the Helsinki Final Accords, the *Charter of Paris* [as well as other documents relating to the CSCE process].' 'Vertrag zwischen der Bundesrepublik Deutschland und der Republik Polen über gute Nachbarschaft und freundschaftliche Zusammenarbeit', 18 June 1991, *Bulletin*, Nr.68 (18 June 1991), p.542. More generally, the Germans consider the CSCE to be 'the stability framework for the enlarged Europe' and 'the bracket for the emerging pan-European order in all spheres'; and the *Paris Charter* is viewed as the quasi-constitutional framework for a pan-European system ordered by the principles of democracy, human rights, and the market economy. See Hans-Dietrich Genscher, in note 11, p.92–3; and 'The Future of Europe', 12 July 1991, *Statements and Speeches*, Vol.XIV, No.8, pp.3–4.

26. Helmut Kohl, 'Deutsche-amerikanischer Beitrag zur Stabilität und Sicherheit', 21 May 1991, *Bulletin*, Nr.58 (28 May 1991), p.458.

27. Helmut Kohl, 'Die Rolle Deutschlands in Europa', note 14, p.245.

28. See 'KSZE-Konferenz über wirtschaftliche Zusammenarbeit in Europa. Dokument der Bonner Konferenz', 11 April 1990, *Bulletin*, Nr.46 (19 April 1990), pp.357–62. The role of economic co-operation in the creation of a pan-European security system was

acknowledged in the *Paris Charter* of the CSCE. See 'Charta von Paris fur ein neues Europa. Erklarung des Pariser KSZE-Treffens der Staats- und Regierungschefs', 24 November 1990, *Bulletin*, Nr.137 (24 November 1990), pp.1412-3; Bunderminister für Wirtschaft Helmut Haussmann, 'Neue Chancen und Impulse der West-Ost-Zusammenarbeit', 31 January 1990, *Bulletin*, Nr.20 (2 February 1990), p.162.

29. Helmut Kohl, 'Ein geeintes Deutschland als Gewinn für stabilität und Sicherheit in Europa', 25 May 1990, *Bulletin*, Nr.68 (29 May 1990), p.587. See also Kohl, note 15, p.63; President Richard von Weizsäcker, 'Ansprache des Bundespräsidenten', 9 April 1990, *Bulletin*, Nr.46 (19 April 1990), pp.362–3. Similar sentiments were expressed by Helmut Haussmann, 'Abschlusserklärung des Bundeswirtschaftsminister', 9 April 1990, ibid., p.363; Hans-Dietrich Genscher, 'Rede des Bundesaussenministers', 11 April 1990, ibid., p.365; and Gerhard Stoltenberg, 'Deutsche Einheit und europäische Sicherheit,' 1 May 1990, *Bulletin*, Nr.52 (5 May 1990), p.408.

30. Helmut Kohl, 'KSZE-Wirtschaftskonferenz in Bonn', 19 March 1990, *Bulletin*, Nr.37 (20 March 1990), p.287; and 'Ein geeintes Deutschland als Gewinn für Stabilität und Sicherheit in Europa', note 229, p.589.

31. Hans-Dietrich Genscher, note 11.

32. Helmut Kohl, note 15, p.72; Hans-Dietrich Genscher, note 11, p.91; Gerhard Stoltenberg, 'Das Selbstverständnis des Soldaten in der Bundeswehr von Morgen', note 20, p.566.

33. Helmut Kohl, note 18, p.578; Hans-Dietrich Genscher, 'Bewertung des Ratsvorsitzenden', 20 June 1991, *Bulletin*, Nr.72 (22 June 1991), p.584.

34. 'Deutschland, Frankreich und Polen in der Verantwortung für Europas Zukunft. Gemeinsame Erklärung der Aussenminister von Deutschland, Frankreich und Polen in Weimar', 29 August 1991, *Bulletin*, Nr.92 (3 September 1991), p.735. The German position was embraced by the Community. The Luxembourg European Council Meeting communiqué of June 1991 stated that, 'The European Council considers the creation of a European economic space to be an essential element of the future architecture of Europe.' See 'Europäischer Rat in Luxembourg', 29 June 1991, *Bulletin*, Nr.78 (9 July 1991), p.625.

35. Gerhard Stoltenberg, note 10, p.655.

36. Helmut Kohl, note 15, p.72.

37. Hans-Dietrich Genscher, 'Sicherheitspolitische Fragen eines künftigen geeinten Deutschland', 19 February 1990, *Bulletin*, Nr.28 (21 February 1990), p.218.

38. See the comments of Gerhard Stoltenberg, 'Das Selbstverständnis des Soldaten in der Bundeswehr von morgen', note 20. Finance Minister Waigel has stated the need for European union in starker terms: 'The world needs a single Europe as an world economic and world political stability factor.' Theodor Waigel, 'Haushaltsgesetz 1992 vor dem Deutschen Bundestag', 3 September 1991, *Bulletin*, Nr.93 (4 September 1991), p.747.

39. Helmut Kohl, note 17, p.513.

40. Chancellor Kohl was unable to press the German claim that the EC should become primarily responsible for asylum and immigration policy at the EC Maastricht summit. The Maastricht participants did consider moving asylum policy to the EC at the 1993 summit, *Economist*, 14 December 1991, No.7737, p.54.

41. Bundesminister des Innern Wolfgang Schläuble, 'Vorschläge und Bemühungen zur Lösung der Asylproblematik', 7 August 1991, *Bulletin*, Nr.85 (9 August 1991), p.689.

42. 60 per cent of those seeking political asylum in the EC choose Germany. Moreover, the number of those seeking asylum has risen dramatically: in 1978, 33,000 individuals sought asylum in Germany and in 1990, 193,063. And close to 70 per cent of today's asylum seekers come from eastern and south-eastern Europe. The number of Aussiedler (ethnic Germans immigrating to Germany) rose from 54,887 in 1979 to 397,073 in 1990. Moreover, the number of foreign residents in Germany rose from 1.2 per cent of the German population in 1961 to 7.2 per cent in 1991. German Press and Information Office, 'Focus On . . . Foreigners in Germany', mimeo, November 1991, p.3 and Tables I and II.

43. Ibid., p.2.
44. Wolfgang Schäuble, 'Innere Sicherheit und Stabilität der rechtsstaatlichen Demokratie. Erklärung des Bundesministers des Innern zum Verfassungsschutzbericht 1988', 4 July 1989, *Bulletin*, Nr.73 (8 July 1989), p.640.
45. *New York Times*, 16 December 1991, p.A9.
46. These concerns are not unique to the Germans; the French and the British are equally concerned about immigration and border control. The difference, however, is found in Germany's geography and historical experience, which constrain Germany in ways France and Britain are not.
47. Western European Union, *Platform on European Security Interests*, The Hague, 27 October 1987, mimeo.
48. 'Gemeinsame Erklärung anlässlich der 56. deutsche-französischen Konsultationen am 17. und 18. September 1990 in München', 18 September 1990, *Bulletin*, Nr.111 (19 September 1990), p.1170.
49. Helmut Kohl, note 15.
50. Gerhard Stoltenberg, 'Das Selbstverständnis des Soldaten in der Bundeswehr von morgen', note 20.
51. 'Kommunique des Ministerrates der Westeuropäischen Union', 27 June 1991, *Bulletin* (5 July 1991), p.621.
52. 'Europäischer Rat in Luxembourg', 29 June 1991, *Bulletin*, Nr.78 (9 July 1991), p.625; and 'Kommunique der Ministertagung des Nordatlantikrats', 7 June 1991, *Bulletin*, Nr.66 (11 June 1991), p.527; 'Deutschland, Frankreich und Polen in der Verantwortung für Europas Zukunft', note 34, p.734; and note 51.
53. Hans-Dietrich Genscher, speech before the WEU, 8 July 1991, *Statements and Speeches*, Vol.XIV, No.7, p.1.
54. For a detailed statement of the Franco–German proposal, see 'Botschaft zur gemeinsamen europäischen Aussen- und Sicherheitspolitik', 14 October 1991, *Bulletin*, Nr.117 (18 October 1991), pp.929–31. The French and Germans also proposed an expansion of the Franco–German brigade from 5,000 to over 30,000 troops, *New York Times*, 17 October 1991, p.A1.
55. *Economist*, note 40, p.52.
56. It is also the case that the WEU allows the Europeans to side-step the immediate problems associated with Irish (and Austrian and Swedish) neutrality and the longer-term problems associated with the EC membership of former member-states of the Warsaw Pact, particularly Poland, Hungary, and the Czech and Slovak Federal Republic.
57. Helmut Kohl, 'Ein geeintes Deutschland als Gewinn für Stabilität und Sicherheit in Europa', note 29, p.586; on the need for 'self-containment' see also Chef des Bundeskanzleramtes Rudolf Seiters, 'Perspektiven der Deutschlandpolitik im geeinten Europa', 30 November 1990, *Bulletin*, Nr.141 (5 December 1990), p.1485; Helmut Kohl, 'Besuch des Bundeskanzlers in den Vereinigten Staaten von Amerika', 5 June 1990, *Bulletin*, Nr.74 (13 June 1990), p.638.

The Renovation of French Defence Policy

ROBBIN LAIRD

The purpose of this article is to identify the dynamics of change within the French defence community in the wake of the revolution of 1989. The basis of French policy has changed, as has the environment within which the classical defence concept was framed. With a change in the objective basis of policy there is a struggle to provide a new intellectual structure to define defence policy in a way which seems relevant to the France of today, not of yesterday. The Mitterrand administration is seeking to frame policy for the next ten years at a critical juncture in history. By setting the broad framework for the near- to mid-term it hopes to shape the longer-term policy much as de Gaulle did in the mid 1960s.

IMPACT OF CHANGING ENVIRONMENT

The Revolution of 1989

The revolution of 1989 had a cross-cutting impact on French perceptions of the viability of their defence policy. On the one hand, the revolution resonated with the classic assumptions of French defence policy. The blocs would end; the Russians would act more like a great power than an ideological and expansionist one; and European construction would supersede the superpower confrontation within Europe. On the other hand, events seemed to happen too quickly and the American role in Europe was undercut, as well as the traditional west European concept of the European construction process seemed to be overwhelmed.

Reinforcement of Classic Assumptions

The end of the blocs The revolution of 1989 reinforced the classic Gaullist instinct about the end of the blocs, of the building of Europe from the Atlantic to the Urals. The collapse of Soviet control in eastern Europe, the dynamics of change in the USSR, and the acceleration of a comprehensive process of conventional disarmament – all of these factors were leading to the end of the domination by the superpowers over the European construction process.

The role of Russia The Gaullist language focused upon Russia, not the Soviet Union. The end of the Soviet Union as an ideological power with expansionist goals was clearly signalled by the changes of 1989 and 1990. Mitterrand spoke frequently of the role of Russia and the Russians, not of the Soviet Union. The Russians were expected to act like Russians, and to follow classical geopolitical strategy, e.g., resisting the unification of Germany. The French government expected a slow process of unification, largely because of the anticipated Russian refusal to accept it.

European construction versus superpower confrontation   With the apparent end of the superpower domination – by confrontation or condominium – the Europeans (i.e., the west Europeans) were in a position to seize the moment and expand their control over their own destinies. West European development would continue with the Franco-German dyad at the heart, and eastern Europe would be gradually associated with the new, dynamic, 'greater' Europe.

Challenges to Classic Assumptions

The American role   Mitterrand has from the beginning of his Presidency been an 'Atlanticist'. His position has been clearly stated at various moments of his Presidency, notably in November 1988 and April 1991. In 1988 he underscored in a major speech before the Institute of Higher Defence Studies (IHEDN) that the Americans are the key ally of France. In 1991 he reiterated the significance of the American role before the defence forum at the French Military School.

The Americans readily embraced the new opportunities in the wake of the revolution of 1989 and the French administration worried that the Americans might leave Europe too quickly, and thereby undercut the European construction process. The Americans are perceived to be critical to nurturing further success in the Europeanization effort, but the adminstration has been at odds over how best to deal with the United States and Europe simultaneously.

The concept of European development   Simultaneously with the challenge to the transatlantic relationship, the revolution of 1989 threatened the process of west European construction. By becoming unhinged rapidly from the classic East–West confrontation, the east Europeans began to clamour for their place at the European table. But they were not Europeans – at least not all of them – and, by too rapidly broadening it, the community's process of development would be subverted. France might be itself unhinged from the process of European construction for which it had so long worked. Monnet, it must be remembered, is at least as important as de Gaulle in shaping the European synthesis within which post-war French policy has been shaped. The French leadership within the west European construction effort has always been high and remains so – Delors and Attali are French after all and part of the Mitterrand adminstration's definition of the future of Europe.

Noise distortion or paradigmatic challenge? Were the challenges to the classic Gaullist definition of French defence and security policy simply bumps in the path ahead or challenges requiring a paradigmatic shift? It would only be with the twin impacts of German unification and the Gulf War that this question would be clearly decided in favour of renovation. But what would not remain clear was how much renovation would be needed. Could France frame a new nationalist policy or did it need to reframe its entire definition of national participation in the West and within Europe?

Unification of Germany

Centrality to French Approach

The unification process happened much more quickly than the French expected. On the basis of interviews conducted in 1990, it was clear that the French administration believed the SPD would win the elections in March 1990 in the GDR. This victory would work as a strategic asset of the Soviets, and the Russians would work for a gradual process of change. The challenge for the West and for France would be to provide as much room for manoeuvre as possible for West Germany as it dealt with the unification process.

With the acceleration of the unification process, the French administration had to adjust its policy and to sort out its instincts toward the building of a common policy with the new Germany. For the French, the Germans are central to the former's defining of their own role within Europe. From a negative standpoint, the French's coping with German policy is at stake. From a positive standpoint, the challenge is to find ways to work together to define west European foreign and security policy.

Partner?

Would the new Germany be a partner with France as the old West Germany had been? Was there a psychology of national renewal that would lead to German national egoism and an inability to work psychologically with the other Europeans? In private conversations, Mitterrand referred to Chancellor Kohl as perhaps the last European German chancellor. He has been concerned to find ways through the Genscher–Dumas relationship and his own relationship with Kohl to adapt the old dyad to new conditions.

Competitor?

Would the new Germany define its role in a more adversarial manner? Would it seek to become an overtly national competitor with France? Would such nationalism torpedo the west European construction process? The President decided to deal with this problem by trying to maintain this construction process, and indeed to accelerate it if possible. This meant deflecting east European pressure to expand the Community; the confederation idea was developed in part to do this. This meant pressuring the Germans to continue the monetary unification process, even in the face of serious economic difficulties for the West Germans in incorporating the East Germans.

There are also clear fears that the Soviet–German relationship on the one hand, and the American–German relationship on the other would augment Germany's place in Europe at the expense of the European construction process. The Soviet–German treaty in September 1990 underscored French concerns about the undue influence of the Soviets on German security policy. The German performance in the Gulf War only reinforced it. On the other hand, the privileged partnership which Secretary Baker has sought to create between the USA and Germany has only enhanced French fears of exclusion. If the special relationship with Britain continues (and was evident again in the Gulf War), and if there is a privileged relationship between the USA and Germany, what is the role of France in American policy toward Europe?

Immobilism?

Even before the Gulf War, French officials were seriously concerned with the possibility of German immobilism. Would the preoccupation by Germany with its own development subvert the German ability to create a new Europe, a Europe in which the Franco–German dynamic would remain central?

Notably, the greatest gap between public discourse and private governmental thinking revolves around the immobilism issue. For French intellectuals the most often noted fear is of a new Germany, arrogant and strong. For high-ranking French officials the concern is with the collapse of a vigorous Germany capable and willing of playing a solid role in building the new Europe.

The Gulf War

No factor has been of greater significance in pushing the French over the barrier to discussing the necessity for change than the Gulf War. One could write and, indeed, needs to write an assessment of the ongoing debate within France over the 'lessons of the Gulf War'. These lessons are decidedly political and will be used in the upcoming debate about the future of French defence and security policy. Simply an enumeration of some key impacts will be given here.

Coalition-Building as a Natural Alliance Dynamic

A number of French officials noted that the Americans built a coalition to deal with the Iraqi threat outside NATO and not within it. They used their relations with the British and the French to co-ordinate policy; with the Western European Union to use bases in southern Europe; and with 'Western-oriented' Arabs to legitimize a multinational effort. This is treated as the norm in out-of-Europe actions, and, more significantly, this *ad hoc* effort will be more and more the case even when dealing with direct European defence issues in the period ahead. With the end of the direct Soviet threat against the West, it will be impossible – except in extreme circumstances – to mount a completely integrated and co-ordinated response to European security challenges in advance. Rather the task will be to reinforce the organs of political and military co-ordination (not integration) to deal with the global problems challenging the Western Alliance.

Salience of Military Co-ordination

Notable in the language of the administration is the emphasis upon co-ordination, not integration. Military integration is a *bête noire* for the French, but co-ordination is not. The Gulf 'showed the importance of having exercised forces in common within the Alliance, but it does not justify the continued existence of a tightly co-ordinated SHAPE', a very high-ranking French military official commented.

The Nature of Modern Warfare

The performance of the new technologies and the new concepts of the American forces (notably air-land battle) have finally brought home to French officials and the public that the old style of warfare is *passé*. It is not enough to have tanks, airplaines and isolated pieces of military equipment. Modern warfare is integrated and systems-oriented. Command, control and communication and modern forms of intelligence are indispensable in knitting together forces to fight in a modern way. Although there is an overwhelming consensus on this point, there are differences to be drawn concerning the impact on specific French forces (but this debate is only now beginning in earnest and will be an integral component of the concurrent debate about the 'lessons of the Gulf' and about the new military programme law to be introduced in the fall of 1992).

The Impact of Proliferation

The President has clearly and decisively argued that France must not stand back as in the past from dealing with the question of arms proliferation. There is no clearly agreed upon agenda within the government on how to deal with this problem, but there is a clear desire to do so.

The Inadequacy of French Forces

In spite of official self-praise for the French performance, virtually all high-ranking military officials underscore the inadequacy of French forces to fight in a modern war. They argue not only for changing the nature of those forces but over how to participate more effectively with other Western forces, including the Americans.

KEY DOMESTIC PRESSURES FOR REASSESSMENT

Economic Growth

Slow growth is a critical factor undercutting Western defence establishments. France is no different. The French defence budget has been planned to operate in a relatively high growth environment. Even as officials reassessed the growth environment necessary for a serious defence effort, their estimates were too high. The 1991 budget was planned within a modest overall economic growth of 2.6 per cent. This target figure was not met, which pressured the defence budget even more than had been anticipated (overall economic growth between 1985 and 1991 is indicated in Figure 1).

FIGURE 1
ANNUAL FRENCH GDP GROWTH, 1985–1991

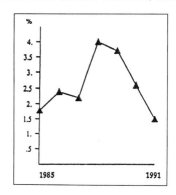

Source: French government

The impact of declining economic growth is significant. Figure 2 attempts to project the impact of various growth projections on shortfalls in total French defence spending. The figure is derived from the data presented in Table 1 below. This has four cells: the first is based on the projected growth in the budgetary planning process; the other three are based on variant budgetary percentages related to the current growth rate of 1.5 per cent. The difference between the variant percentages could yield a gap of as much as 30 billion francs.

TABLE 1
THE IMPACT OF ECONOMIC GROWTH
ON THE DEFENCE BUDGET, 1991

GDP growth (%)	Defence budget (%)	Defence budget in billions of francs
2.6	3.37	194.5
1.5	3.5	194.5
1.5	3.37	187.2
1.5	3.0	166.7

FIGURE 2
THE IMPACT OF ECONOMIC GROWTH ON THE DEFENCE BUDGET, 1991

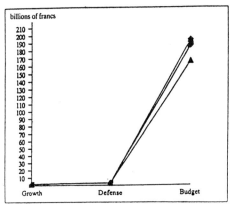

Budgetary Dynamics

The Mitterrand administration has consistently avoided making serious choices within the defence budget as the gap between plan and reality widened. One measure of this gap is contained in Figure 3. What is presented there is the gap between planned and actual expenditures seen from the standpoint of each of the major sections of the budget. The gap is expressed in positive percentages in the chart, but is in reality a measure of a negative percentage gap between the plan and reality.

FIGURE 3
COMPARISON OF PROJECTED EXPENDITURES BETWEEN PROGRAMME LAW
AND ACTUAL EXPENDITURES, 1991

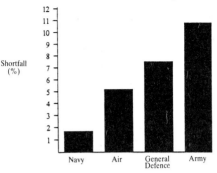

Stretching programmes is the approach of choice for politicians, and it may be adopted once again. Nonetheless, Defence Minister Joxe seems determined to take action for the next multi-year programme law. His predecessor was defeated within French bureaucratic politics last summer in part by failing to get his budget approved. He was clearly not backed by the President and felt increasingly isolated within the French administration.

Arms Industries

Around 95 per cent of French military equipment is provided by indigenous production. The DGA (*Délégation Générale des Armaments*) and the military industries have formed a powerful lobby resisting change. Nonetheless, the dramatic decline in French arms exports and the increasing recognition by political officials of the need for the europeanization or atlanticization of defence industries undercut the classic French policy of the isolation of these industries from external competitive pressures.

Although change is difficult, the reduction in the defence budgets in the West and in deployed forces will shrink the French defence industry along with their Western competitors. Collaboration will be forced by necessity. The fact that this global process affects France as well has not been lost on either industry or government.

Declining Markets

French arms sales have declined precipitously since the mid 1980s. There is no prospect of recovering the old markets, especially with the interest of the administration in dealing with arms proliferation. If there is to be a recovery of the arms markets, it will have to occur through co-operation with American and European industries.

Redefinition of French Miliary Needs

The redefinition of French military needs carries with it a shift in the industrial requirements. Increasingly, French officials understand that those needs cannot be met on a national basis alone.

The Impact of 1992

The impact of the European Common Market is widely recognized to lead to pressures to include defence production within it. Isolation of defence industries through the use of subsidies will increasingly be out of phase with the effort to build European-wide industrial consortia. There is a noticeable difference of view within French defence industry between those firms striving to become competitive on a European scale and those which remain oriented largely toward the French market.

Public Opinion and Defence

Another factor affecting a reassessment is the changing nature of public opinion. French public opinion, like that in other Western democracies, is changing with regard to defence. New cleavages and new issues are emerging which will decisively shape the environment within which defence policy will be made.

The American Factor

French forces went under American command in the Gulf War without much negative reaction from the public. A more permissive relationship with the Americans and the Atlantic Alliance on military co-ordination is clearly possible.

The European Factor

In spite of the good perceptions of the United States currently held, French opinion clearly favours their defence issues being within the European basket, rather than simply reaffirming the old transatlantic Alliance.

Opinion in the Gulf War

Opinion sampled during the Gulf War revealed a number of characteristiscs of contemporary French opinion about defence issues. The most important is the continuing importance of a national defence system, i.e., of the President's being able to define a national defence priority as the key motivator for French intervention. But other opinion data reveal that it is a national priority seen in trust for Europe, or of having significance for Europe as a whole.

The Political Salience of Foreign Policy

Other opinion data reveal – not surprisingly – the centrality of foreign policy for the President and his party's standing in public opinion. This simply reinforces the perceived necessity to have national forces available to serve foreign policy goals defined to meet national objectives. Put in other terms, the restructuring of French forces will be done both to deal with the domestic situation and to provide tools to try to influence the process of change in the western Alliance. A composite of French attitudes may be seen in Figure 4.

FIGURE 4
FRENCH PERCEPTIONS OF THEMSELVES, THE AMERICANS AND OF THE
EUROPEAN DYNAMIC IN THE GULF CRISIS

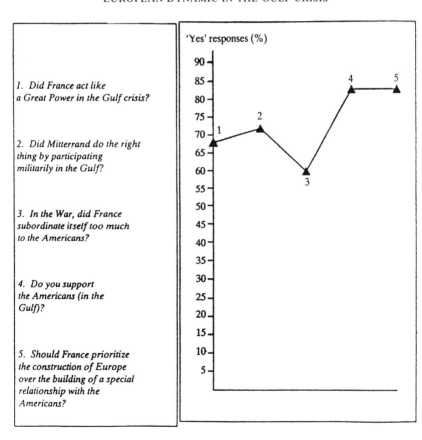

Source: data from polls carried out by *L'Express* and *Le Point* in February and March 1991.

Defining Reassessment

It is extremely important to be clear about how the French administration and the defence community look at the reassessment dynamic. There are two basic instincts. For some, reassessment is an examination of how classic Gaullist policy may be maintained in different conditions. For others, reassessment is a process of reconceptualizing the place of France's defence and security policy within the new European and transatlantic frameworks. What has happened is a moving consensus, in the sense of a shift in the plausibility structure of thought legitimizing a national political structure. Basic structures must be adjusted; the differences are over how much and in what manner.

FRENCH MILITARY FACTORS

The Challenge

The key challenge for the administration is that change is occurring in all key dimensions of defence policy at once. Conflict within the Socialist Party and between the Socialists and the Conservatives will place a premium upon making strategic change from below not above.

The Nuclear Factor

One of the most important impacts of the revolution of 1989 and of the Gulf War was to reduce the perceived importance of nuclear weapons. These weapons of last resort remain useful to deter the Russians from adventurism, but not much else. They are useful in the long term to deflect pressure from Third World states in any attempt to use nuclear weapons to blackmail Europe; but this is not a short-term proposition. France must remain a nuclear power, but increasingly at less cost.

The most immediate question is the future of the nuclear 'triad'. The key players in the administration have already decided against maintaining a triad, and the debate has shifted to the question of what will be the second component of the strategic forces. Notably, the key question is whether to build an air-launched missile for the strategic forces. The President is leaning toward delaying this decision until the follow-on question for the ASMP (tactical air-to-surface missile) becomes more pressing. Also, he would like to have British participation in the programme but he knows that this will not be possible without the re-election of the Conservative Party in 1992. Without the Tories, the ASLP (the long-range variant of the ASMP) can only be a French programme.

The 'New Defence Imperative'

Both the President and the Defence Minister are keenly aware that defence efforts must be linked with the future and not just the past. That is why they have focused upon space and C³I as the key elements of the 'new defence imperative'. The new technologies are linked with the American success in the Gulf, and the building of a European defence, and provide symbolism as important to future efforts as the nuclear programme has been in the past.

Defence Minister Joxe is clearly focusing upon military space as the crown jewel of the new military programme law. He underscored in his first interviews and speeches the priority of space, and has already put together an informal team of advisers to shape a new space effort.

The Conventional Forces

For the President, the role of conventional forces is to provide him with a political instrument to exercise French influence, not as a component of a collective Western military machine. Reflections on the lessons of the war in the Gulf have even intensified this predisposition. Unhappiness with the military effort in the Gulf will lead to an attempt to create a more effective global instrument of military power, not to a reinforcement of the NATO military effort.

The Army

The plans for the Army will be vigorously debated, but the thinking of the closest military advisers focuses upon a smaller, more professional Army capable of more effective long-range intervention. The transformation of the French Army into a more mobile force is envisaged with a reduction in the size of the total forces. With the forward defence requirements of the Alliance reduced by Soviet withdrawal from eastern Europe, the French Army will engage much further forward in a crisis. These requirements merge with expected requirements for a French intervention out-of-Europe, either with or without allied participation. The tension between European and out-of-Europe demands on the French Army is thereby reduced and made more congenial to French preferences. Professionalization will be important so that the President has more direct control over the instrument of military intervention.

The FAR (Rapid Action Force) was considered to be too light to be useful in the 'Desert Storm' deployment. As a result, the French are considering the formation of a heavy tank division exclusively from professional soldiers. This would be created from the three tank divisions previously based in the Federal Republic of Germany and in the process of returning to French territory.

Conscription will be maintained as a principle, but service time will be reduced to ten months and then perhaps to six. The cost of shifting from conscription to more professionalization is considered to be high, but a number of French defence officials privately indicate that the costs of conscription are much higher than has generally been believed. Notably, the cost of keeping such a large number of garrison posts throughout the country represents an important hidden factor in the defence budget. Whether the current administration has the stomach to take on this issue is another matter, but it is important to the process of real change. The Army will clearly be reduced if the European security environment continues to be relatively benign. By the year 2005, the Army could be reduced to about 180,000 men (approximately 100,000 less than today). A tentative overview of the evolution of the French Army is presented in Table 2.

TABLE 2
THE CHANGING STRUCTURE OF THE FRENCH ARMY

	1990 Figures	Army 2000 Plan Targets	2005 Options
Army manpower	285,000	250,000	150–180,000* 2 corps?
Army structure	3 corps	2 corps	(FAR plus mobile tank division)
French forces in Germany (FFA)	3 divisions	1 division	?

Note: * Need deployable force of 30,000, which requires at least a 150,000-man level.

The Air Force

A number of key reflections about the future of the Air Force have been generated by the Gulf War. First, the Air Force was unable to deploy its *Mirage* 2000Ns to the Kuwait theatre of operations. They could have been transformed into a conventional version in a matter of weeks by using the system of adaptation referred to as 'Kit K2'. The military claims that the political leadership failed to give the order and the political leadership claims that the Air Force Chief of Staff dragged his feet.

Second, the Air Force fought with aircraft which could not fly at night. The British flew European aircraft which performed well in all-weather conditions, but the French pilots could only watch the others operate in these conditions. The Air Force is fuming over its inability to participate more fully owing to inadequate equipment.

In addition, the nature of modern air war underscored how out-of-phase of the French concept of air operations has been. The central place of command, control and intelligence was starkly pointed out by the realities of the American Air Force's performance in the Gulf War.

Also the French Air Force had inadequate supplies of ammunition. Ironically, the French built an excellent laser-guided missile used by the allies in the war, but the French themselves had very few available for their own use, according to French authorities.

The impact of all of these factors has been to reinforce the instinct of the political authorities to build a smaller, but more capable air arm. Again, the concern will be to have this force capable of operating over much greater distances than is now possible.

The Navy

The main debate generated about the Navy by the Gulf War surrounds the aircraft carrier. The inadequate performance of the French carriers in the War has raised the issue of the role of such an expensive power-projection tool. Because of its high cost and its inadequacy in a national context, several French officials are now arguing that it would be better to adopt the British solution or to eliminate the carrier altogether. In addition, some military officials are arguing that the Air Force could provide the necessary power projection role in the Mediterranean.

The debate about the carrier quickly becomes a debate about the French role in the world. Increasingly, French officials are considering the withdrawal of their out-of-Europe interests to Africa, the western Mediterranean and, perhaps, the Middle East. If they were so limited, there is no obvious necessity for the fixed-wing aircraft carrier, or perhaps for a carrier at all.

FRANCE IN THE NEW MULTINATIONAL ENVIRONMENT

General Perspectives on France in the New Security Environment

What is most striking about the tone, style and substance currently within the Mitterrand administration is the emphasis on the need for reassessment and the enhancement of France's role in the new international environment. The shock of events in the past three years has led to a kind of immobilism common within the Alliance from an inability to define clearly the path ahead and the preferred options within the sweep of history. But within the administration one can see very different nuances or emphases upon the paths of change; each can be identified with a different French political figure.

Delors

Delors represents the administration's perspective on the European construction process. For Delors, security policy must be added as a component of the political consultative process within the EC. He is very flexible about how this is done, but not that it must be done. He has been quite vocal about the failure of 'Europe' to play a role in the Gulf War, by which he means the EC and its political consultative organs. The role of the European Council in shaping a 'European response' to the Kurdish issue is an illustration of the 'new' role for Europe generated under his leadership.

Also, Delors has launched an effort to build a security-assessment capability within the Commission. The role of France is to build a Europe in which western European construction is accelerated, the east Europeans are gradually associated and assimilated, and the Americans play a key role in supporting, nurturing and participating in the Western economic and political construction process. Over time, security issues predominate over defence issues, and become adjuncts to the processes of economic and political consultation and co-operation. Defence capabilities are part of the crisis management system within Europe.

Attali

Attali represents the pro-European wing of the Socialist Party which places little long-term value on the relationship with the United States. The transatlantic relationship was once critical, but represents a phase of history in which the United States was essential in order to deflect Soviet military power. With the Russians becoming less of a military superpower and more of a declining great power, they can become partners in the building of the new Europe. The new European Bank is seen by Attali to serve primarily the purpose of stitching the Russians and the remnants of the Soviet empire into the 'new Europe', and is less of an instrument for east European reconstruction and development to the exclusion of the Russians. France's role is to nurture a new multinational system in Europe within which the Russians may play a more normal role, and the Americans are subordinated to the new European colossus.

Mitterrand

Mitterrand is the most vocal Atlanticist within the Socialist Party. His Atlanticism is rooted in the experience of World War II and the cold war. It represents the past more than the future and raises the question of the problem of generational change. How will Atlanticism be revalidated in the future rather than simply being a relic of the past?

The President is always complicated to interpret, but he has a very strong propensity for multilateral solutions to international issues. He sees France's role as helping to build the new Europe (certainly along lines of national preference) and not emphasizing national solutions outside the multinational context. The frequent comparisons made between de Gaulle and Mitterrand miss this important point of contrast; de Gaulle rebuilt the French sense of themselves in the world via a new nationalism; Mitterrand sees his vocation as building a new Europe within which France remains a significant force for the future.

As a result, the President's focus upon multialteralism is multifaceted. The Americans remain important because they are a big power congenial to western European development and must be included in the European construction process. The President's own proclivities would favour a deepening of co-operation among the 'serious' players in Western defence, and his instincts might be to promote a new form of the directorate on nuclear matters and new forms of co-operation within the Alliance on a host of defence and security issues. But the relationship with the Americans and on defence reassessments must not undercut the European construction process. It is necessary to find ways to co-operate within western Europe and to find ways to converse with the East to enhance European development, not to undercut it.

The Future of the Western Alliance: Basic Approaches within the French Administration

The only true point of consensus within the French defence and security community is the belief that the broad concept of the Alliance which the French have defined in the past remains valid. Rather than equating the Alliance with the NATO military machinery, the French have pursued a broad political approach toward the Alliance. This approach is seen to be validated by events but, as indicated throughout this article, there is a serious reassessment of how this approach should be modified for the new international situation.

The administration's approach to the reform of NATO is in reality two approaches. There is a conservative approach which emphasizes keeping things like they are for as long as it is feasible, and a reformist approach which underscores the need for change both at the NATO and the French level. The conflict between these two orientations creates not only tension within the administration but, if unresolved by the President, will lead to immobilism.

The Conservative Approach or an Emphasis upon Institutional Maintenance

The conservative approach (within the administration) rests upon three assumptions which are not necessarily held by all who support this approach. These assumptions all reinforce the propensity to maintain the classic role of France within the Alliance as well as the institutional setting of NATO.

Maintain an American Presence as a Buffer For a number of advocates of caution, the American presence remains critical in the period of transition in Europe. The Americans are useful to counterbalance the Russians; and there is no real European defence organization on the horizon. Rather than offend the Americans by pushing for 'real' reform, it is better to try to develop a privileged position on a bilateral basis. The longstanding French position of being within the political organs of NATO but outside the military ones is viewed as still valid.

Wait and See and Keep France 'Independent' The current state of the Western alliance is uncertain and unstable. Eventually change will come and France should keep its 'independent' position until the outlines of 'real' changes are much clearer than they are now. France should not throw its limited influence into a process of reform, because of the lack of clarity in East–West and transatlantic relations. France should build its national capabilities now for a future effort to construct a new alliance within Europe.

Atrophy and Regeneration The basic approach of the advocate of institutional maintenance is to observe the process of atrophy of Western defence institutions and to find the appropriate moment to seek to regenerate a collective effort. Advocates of this position are not really narrow-minded nationalists; rather they are simply unwilling to gamble on the creation of something new now. It is better to preserve what France and the Alliance have attained rather than to try to regenerate the French and Alliance approaches to common defence and security.

Bilateralism For advocates of this approach, change will come as bilateral linkages within the West and between western states and eastern Europe and parts of the former Soviet Union are deepened. Rather than try to adapt NATO or to create a new system, it is better to keep the old and to form new relationships outside that system through bilateral channels. The east Europeans should be kept out of NATO, but bilateral relations between west and east Europe should be encouraged in defence and security affairs.

The Reformist Approach or Institutional Adaptation

For proponents of institutional adaptation, there is a strong belief that the security system of the West is inherently unstable. With no clear enemy, public support will decline over time in support of strong defence efforts. With the emergence of a unified Germany, the classic convergence of interests among the Western states on defence and security issues will collapse. Without a reinvigorated Western system of collective defence, the Russian–German relationship over time will allow the Germans to dominate Western defence and replacement with a pure collective security system. Reinvigoration can come only with institutional change both at the NATO and French levels of participation within NATO.

The Role of NATO   NATO must be reformed; this is certainly a reason for French participation in the NATO review. For proponents of change, the emphasis is upon downplaying the role of SHAPE and SACEUR and increasing the role of the military committee. SACEUR would become less of a Supreme Allied Commander than a Supreme Allied Co-ordinator of military policy. Military co-ordination and planning to meet a diversity of threats and to deal with a range of risks would supersede the emphasis upon integration to meet a single threat from the East. The Alliance approach upon deterrence would shift and an emphasis upon a broad political management of crisis.

For advocates of change, the necessity to build a European rapid deployment force is a key opportunity to build a lever for institutional adaptation. A European RDF would be built by stitching together national modular units. In the process, a planning staff and command element would be developed. The military leaders who would emerge in this effort would form the nucleus of a European SACEUR. Also, the requirement to rotate forces throughout the Alliance and to reduce the emphasis upon exercises upon German soil could be met through the European RDF. For example, even significant contingents of German soldiers could be deployed to France on a regular rotational basis. German soldiers wearing European hats and badges are a much more welcome force than German soldiers wearing only German uniforms.

The Role of European Institutions within the Alliance   Reform of NATO is a necessary but not sufficient condition for change within the system of Western collective defence. There must be a greater effort to europeanize the Alliance, not only within but from without. As the Europeans play a greater role over time within NATO institutions, there will be a blending with other institutions, notably with the Western European Union and the security policy efforts of the European Community.

The French Role or the Nature of 'Independence'   Change in the

Alliance requires a French role, but this role cannot be played if France remains aloof from the processes of change. France could enter the NATO military committee, if changes in the meaning of military integration were made. With an emphasis upon co-ordination, the Alliance could build the integration for the 'new' Alliance. France's 'independence' in defence and security affairs has meaning only so as to influence the process of adapting Western defence and security institutions to changing conditions.

CONCLUSION

The French Case: How Unique?

The dynamics of change analysed in this article are both unique to France and generally related to a process of change in the Western defence system. How unique is the French case and how do the dynamics of change within France relate to the pressures for change in the West as a whole?

The unique qualities of transition relate to the adaptation of and challenges to the specific French defence paradigm of the Fifth Republic. Specifically, the challenge is to adapt the meaning of 'independence' to new conditions, to find a new bargain with the Germans for west European construction, to come to terms with the transatlantic relationship with the Americans, and to try to influence the West's approach toward eastern Europe and the CIS. A full examination of each of these processes of change is beyond the scope of this article, but they all in their own way undercut the foundation of the classic French defence synthesis. In this sense, the French face a unique problem of adaptation.

General Dynamics

But seen from the standpoint of the pressures for transition within the Alliance as a whole, the French case seems less unique. Each of the major states in the Alliance with strong defence capabilities faces a set of challenges to the foundations of its postwar defence and security policy. Each in its own way faces four broad alternatives.

Downsizing

In each of the key states, there are significant political forces which wish to keep the Alliance as it is and to simply reduce the national contribution parallel to a total Alliance reduction. The Alliance will be reconfigured with forces at a lower level, but will still look somewhat like it does today in ten years' time.

Revalidating collective defence

Reformers in each Western state value the collective defence experience of the past 40 years, but argue that the institutions which expressed that experience must be modified. Serious differences exist among reformers concerning the scope, pace and nature of change necessary to revalidate collective defence within the western Alliance, but the emphasis is upon adaptation to a new global environment.

Renationalization

But an inability to adapt the Alliance to new conditions may simply see individual states in the Alliance taking unilateral decisions concerning their forces and the strategies to use them. In effect, unilateralism leads to a renationalization process within Europe in defence policy. Such an approach is simply out of phase with the requirements of European construction and will become an important impediment to further development of the political construction process.

Collective security

For others, the defence problem will be transformed in the European construction process. Military forces will look more like an adjunct to police actions and as means to enforce collective security decisions rather than an independent factor shaping the future of Europe. Advocates of the CSCE as the main organ for the development of a new European security policy are to be found in France as elsewhere in Europe. There is a strong collective security element within the Socialist Party which will become more visible in the post-Mitterrand period.

The French Paths

Paralysis

One possible path ahead will be paralysis in French defence policy. This could occur as a result of an inability to resolve serious conflicts within the administration or between the administration and its political rivals. The style of Mitterrand might lead to this result, because without a strong assertion of a new agenda a stasis of bureaucracy might overwhelm the reform instinct. Also, without clear allies outside France for reform – notably without support from the Americans and the Germans for some form of NATO reform congenial to the reform caucus in France – stasis will be reinforced, which, in turn, will reinforce immobilism and paralysis.

Renationalization

Renationalization could occur through a failure to reform and a reassertion of the validity of classic Gaullist policy in new conditions. Here the French would seek to see a looser western Alliance emerge in which the key states of the Alliance co-operated – especially on a European bilateral and multilateral level – to promote national objectives. One often hears French political leaders talk about the desirability of the Germans becoming more assertive nationally – including on military issues – but it is simply hard to believe that this talk accurately reflects how the French public would react to German renationalization on defence and security issues. Thus the limits of this French position are reached with consideration of the importance of European construction to French policy. Renationalization would be a sign of failure not the triumph of the Gaullist model on a European scale.

Reform

The specific French reform variant has been sketched out throughout this article. The reformers are found in key positions in the Elysée and the Ministry of Defence. They will seek allies abroad in their effort to draw France out of its relative isolation on defence issues. Without reform in NATO and in the European defence system it will be virtually impossible for serious change in French policy to occur. We may be facing a 'catch-22' situation, in which the weakness of a reform caucus throughout the West leads to a collapse of the reform effort within France.

Apparent Continuity

The most likely course, because it is the easiest to imagine, would be maintenance of French policy along existing lines and simpy reduced to meet budgetary and political requirements. It would only be apparent continuity because the economic and budgetary pressures are too great to maintain the French defence effort on an effective basis in the decade ahead.

In short, the success or failure of a French reform effort will be reflective of and contribute to the processes of change within the Alliance as a whole. Both the French and the broader Alliance effort are only beginning and warrant close attention in the years ahead.

British Approaches to the European Security Debate

STUART CROFT

INTRODUCTION

The British debate over security in the early 1990s has been rather different in nature and scope from that of ten years before. In the early 1980s, the debate focused on nuclear weapons, was articulated by a breakdown in consensus between the Conservative government and the Labour opposition, and mobilized hundreds of thousands of people to demonstrate on the streets of the major British cities while creating heated debate at all levels of British society.[1] Ten years later, the security debate now focuses on questions of political stability and peacekeeping rather than on nuclear weapons, in the context of a new defence consensus between the Conservative government and the Labour opposition, and is the subject of public indifference outside the columns of the quality press.[2] Part of the reason for this change is, of course, the altered strategic environment. But a large proportion of the explanation may be found in the implications of and reactions to the resignation of Margaret Thatcher as Prime Minister.[3] This article will seek to demonstrate this proposition, and then try to examine the implications in relation to the debates in Britain over a European Community security identity, and over the possibility for peacekeeping in Yugoslavia.

However, before we examine British views on European defence co-operation, it is useful to ask the question: what is meant by Europe? For there is a tension in British policy in this area, a division between a security focus and a foreign policy focus. In security terms, Europe means western Europe from most British perspectives. British policy makers and analysts have been loath, for example, even to consider possibilities for the deployment of military force in the Yugoslav/Croatian conflict; and virtually no one gives serious credence to possibilities of extending NATO coverage to central Europe – to Poland, the Czech and Slovak Federal Republic, and Hungary. Yet in foreign policy terms, British policy makers and spokesmen are happy to talk, as Prime Minister Major did in Paris in early September 1991, of a European Community of 30 members, including central Europeans, east Europeans and those nations emerging from the former Soviet Union. At a time when many in Europe are giving consideration to the formation of a European

Community defence/security identity, this says much about the almost consensual view in the United Kingdom about the inappropriateness of a tight defence role for the European Community, as was illustrated in the United Kingdom in the debates over the nature and the implications of the decisions taken at the Maastricht summit.

THE LEGACY OF THATCHERISM

Yet any discussion of the current British attitude to European security must be placed in the context of the legacy of Thatcherism.[4] This is true in three respects: first in terms of the United Kingdom's political relationship with its European Community neighbours – and particularly France and Germany – on the one hand, and with the United States on the other; secondly, in terms of the impact upon the Conservative Party, with its implications for the timing of the 1992 general election and for the future unity of the Party; and thirdly, in terms of the effect on the British Labour Party, and the return to consensual bipartisan politics in security affairs.

It will be argued here that Anglo-West European/United States relations have moved through three periods since the fall of the Berlin Wall: these will be termed trauma, recovery and test. The first period, that of trauma, was characterized by a confusion of purpose and direction as the cold war collapsed, and the bases of Britain's security and foreign policy were undermined. This was a period of hostility to German unification on the part of Britain. Prime Minister Thatcher allowed it to be known that she wanted to slow the process – particularly in January 1990 – and provoked a rift in Anglo-German relations which almost came to public confrontation at the Koenigswinter Anglo-German meeting in March 1990.[5] This was exacerbated by a fear in London – articulated by many prominent journalists writing for newspapers such as *The Independent* and *The Times* – that the end of the cold war would lead to the Anglo-American special relationship being replaced in importance and influence in European and global affairs by the German-American relationship. Further, Mrs Thatcher's attitude to the other west European governments over the ten years of her premiership meant that the United Kingdom had few obvious friends in the European Community, and that a new Anglo-French *entente* to offset growing German power – a relationship spoken of warmly by many in London and Paris during the winter of 1989 and the spring of 1990 – never had a real chance of developing.[6] Certainly the perception on the pro-European wing of the Conservative Party – articulated persuasively by Michael Heseltine – was that Mrs Thatcher had led Britain into a foreign policy cul-de-sac, and that the disarray would have been much greater had it not been for the skill of Douglas Hurd, the Foreign Secretary. Thus one of the immediate foreign policy tasks of John Major when he was elected Prime Minister by Conservative Members of Parliament was to manoeuvre Britain back into the mainstream of European politics and to recover some influence. In this he was assisted by the outbreak, nature and outcome of the Gulf War and the significant role that it enabled Britain to play.

The second period, then, was the recovery of British relations with western Europe under the management of Major and Hurd. The Gulf War seemed to illustrate the continued vitality of the Anglo-American special relationship where questions of military security were concerned, the ability of Britain and France to work together, and it also appeared to highlight the continuing limits to German power, and consequently the limits to the role that any German-American relationship would be able to play.[7] British distaste for Germany's lack of commitment to the conflict was clear in London for much of the war itself, although Major took an opportunity to visit Bonn and to improve greatly the tone of the Anglo-German relationship. But the period of recovery is giving way to one in which British policy will be put to the test. There is widespread concern about the nature of the decisions taken at the Maastricht European Community summit in December 1991 about both economic/monetary and political union. The task for John Major and Douglas Hurd has been to attempt to constrain both agreements in such a fashion that they were able to feel able to sign – and subsequently ratify and implement – the agreements.

This has been complicated, however, by the second legacy of Thatcherism. Mrs Thatcher's high-profile stance on the issue of Europe and her hostility to any form of political integration entrenched disagreements within the Conservative Party: it was the issue on which Sir Geoffrey Howe denounced government policy in his speech resigning from the post of Deputy Prime Minister; it was one of the two main issues on which Michael Heseltine challenged Mrs Thatcher for the leadership of the party and the government. There is a strong pro-European wing in the party; but also a strong anti-European faction. Reconciling the two over Maastricht beyond the general election will be extremely difficult.

The third effect of Thatcherism has been to lead to a major re-examination by the Labour Party of all aspects of its policy. Labour no longer seeks Britain's unilateral nuclear disarmament; indeed, if it were involved in arms control negotiations, the party is now not even prepared to negotiate British nuclear systems away unless all the other nuclear powers do the same.[8] Labour has also reversed its hostility towards the

European Community – Jacques Delors certainly had an important hand in this – to a position broadly indistinguishable from that of John Major. The longevity of Thatcherism has therefore had the effect, in part, of reimposing bipartisanship upon the British security debate.

What, then, are the elements of this bipartisanship? There are essentially two: a commitment to NATO; and a belief in the inability of the West to be able to impose peace in the eastern part of the European continent. NATO is seen to be important for the traditional reasons. There is still concern about the level of armaments inside Russia, although there is little fear that such weapons will be set rolling westward. NATO also offers some element of stability in the new Europe, and it is argued that the Alliance is recognized as providing such a role by the governments of east and central Europe. The Alliance provides some level of insurance against potential threats to the Mediterranean countries, and possibly offers the prospect of being the basis – in terms of experience and logistics, if not necessarily formally – for any future Gulf-style intervention. Above all, the Alliance provides a pivot around which to manage and conceptualize a positive relationship between the United States and western Europe. The influence, equipment, and resources of the United States are still much valued in the United Kingdom as contributions to the creation of a new and stable order in Europe. Thus although great changes have occurred, there is still an important role for NATO. It is accepted, however, that NATO must be adapted, largely by increasing the impact of European states on the organization, and by linking security requirements with the general political desire to construct a greater whole in western Europe.

EUROPEAN STRUCTURES AND PEACEKEEPING

Yet the tasks for which this new adaptation must be designed are seen to be limited. There can, from the British viewpoint, be no role for Western force in imposing peace upon disparate and divergent countries and groups to the east and south-east of Germany. The key fear is of being drawn into a conflict against all sides. The British, with 22 years of experience in attempting to impose peace in Northern Ireland, are well versed in all the drawbacks. Rather than point to the Northern Ireland experience, however, officials have tended to draw parallels with the action in Cyprus in 1974, when 6,000 troops were deployed in a very difficult situation. Multiply the difficulties of Cyprus by – in particular – the complexities of Yugoslavia (if 'Yugoslavia' is still a useful term for that region), and it would require many tens of thousands of troops to be deployed, and a political willingness to accept large casualties over a period of time; certainly more casualties over a longer period of time than the Gulf conflict exacted.

The debate over peacekeeping roles has focused the discussion on to the European Community, and on the arguments for and against a security role for the European Community. The British consensus on this is a strong one, albeit with shades of opinion.[9] Much debate has taken place regarding the desirability of the European Community's extending its role in the field of economic and monetary union, and over the desirability and feasibility of further integration of British policy with that of its European Community neighbours. There is much less disagreement over the desirability of moves to deeper political union (only the Liberal Democrats are in favour of what they term 'federalism' in Europe). The broad consensus supports the following propositions. First, that the strengthening of the west European security identity does not necessarily have to revolve around the European Community members. Although further collaboration on foreign policy is seen to be desirable, there should be firm limits set upon the subjects to be considered, and this should be based upon consensus. Further, in these issues there should be no role for the European Commission, with debate being confined to the states. There is in Conversative ranks a great suspicion of the Commission and especially of Jacques Delors, a man, it is often felt, who sees himself incorrectly as the President of Europe. Those issues left outside the European Community mandate should instead be dealt with by the Western European Union, which should be kept as a distinct organization separate from the European Community, and should work closely with NATO. This was an approach that the British government argued for strongly throughout 1991, and largely formed the basis of the Maastricht agreement.

Such an approach, it is felt, has a number of advantages.[10] First, it would act as a basis to encourage the United States to maintain a close involvement in western European security policy, for it is felt that European Community-based approaches to security are treated in a cool fashion by Washington. There is no inevitability about the United States 'leaving Europe', and indeed that would be a very undesirable outcome. Thus a Western European Union-based approach would reduce the prospect for division since, after all, the purpose is to strengthen Western security arrangements. Second, it would avoid compromising the Irish position, and avoid entanglement in complex Greco-Turkish disputes. Finally, such an approach would leave open the possibility for a faster expansion of the European Community to include states in northern, central, eastern and southern Europe. In integrating these countries into, in John Major's words, 'a European Community of 30 nations', the key difficulties would be economic – which will be challenging enough – with the security dilemmas inherent in the militarization of the European Community neatly sidetracked.

Thus from these viewpoints, one may understand more readily Britain's ambivalence regarding the European Community's peacemaking efforts in Yugoslavia. On the one hand, there has been a desire for these efforts to be successful. The violent dissolution of the Yugoslav federation has been viewed as a major challenge to the development of a new stable order in Europe, and if that can be controlled so much the better. The British government has been extremely reluctant to accede to the recognition of Croatia and, to a lesser extent, of Slovenia – certainly more reluctant than Germany – for fear of hastening this process of collapse. On the other hand, there is a belief that basically this is an issue over which the European Community countries can have only a marginal influence, and to hazard military involvement would be to risk adding fuel to the flames. Thus Britain has been cool over European Community peacekeeping efforts in Yugoslavia, and has openly rejected the deployment of British troops to the region, which John Major made absolutely explicit in a visit to The Netherlands in mid-September 1991. The whole question of peace in Yugoslavia is one over which the Labour Party has been remarkably quiet, thus reinforcing the element of bipartisanship on broad security issues now existing in Britain.

There is, of course, an argument to say that the British consensus is mistaken over the Yugoslav dilemma. This suggests that there is a mistaken diagnosis. For most British analysts the conflict has been caused by rival communities living intermingled with one another, with the means of repression lifted, and with historical scores to settle. It is a conflict, then, driven by emotion at least as much if not more that by political will. To enforce any sort of lasting peace on the region would require a process of imposing a new way of thinking on every individual Serb and Croat. Since this would be flying in the face of centuries of history, it would stand very little chance of success. One can feel the influence of 20 years of bitter experience in attempting to resolve the violence in Northern Ireland clearly structuring the response of many in Britain to the Serb-Croat conflict. These opinions are reinforced by the emphasis in newspaper and television reports on the historical rivalry between Serbs and Croats; on their different religions, cultures and background; and on the period of the Second World War. In other words, the best that might be expected is some form of suppression of violence by outside forces; but as the experience of Northern Ireland has shown, such forces tend to become targets themselves, and the human and political cost over the long term can be high.

In contrast, it could be argued that the emphasis has been misplaced by most analysts in Britain. Certainly the historical dimension is an important one; but the current conflict has a different motor: the ambitions of the nationalist Serb leadership. It was they who provoked the political crisis – few in Britain talk of the 'annexation' and repression of Vojvodina and Kosovo – and it was they who escalated political into military conflict, and it was certainly they who escalated further by involving the Yugoslav federal armed forces. It suits these people for the conflict to continue for as long as they are moving forward. This, of course, is not to argue that all Serbian irregulars are controlled by Belgrade; but it is to suggest that both the Serbian leadership and the irregulars share the same strategic end – the creation of what is loosely termed a 'Greater Serbia'. Threats of economic sanctions are relatively meaningless in such turmoil; other means of changing the balance of political forces are required in order to slow the Serbian advance and therefore to give incentives to Serbia to negotiate.

This much is rarely accepted in the United Kingdom. If it is, the immediate response is nearly always: so what? The impossibility of imposing peace by ground forces remains. The Dutch arguments regarding the threat to use military force to support the peacemaking process are rejected on all the above grounds. For Britain in the Yugoslav case – in sharp contrast to the assumptions and practice of the early stages of the Gulf crisis – there is no chance that the threat to impose force could lead to the withdrawal of aggressive forces. Unfortunately this, as far as can be ascertained, ruled out any *consideration* of the escalation of military options short of an imposition of ground forces. Such measures could have included: the projection of naval forces to lift the blockade of Split, the imposition of an air exclusion zone over Croatia (and Slovenia) to lift the pressure of aerial attack, and to the elimination of the bulk of the Yugoslav federal air force. Such efforts would have been designed to force the Serbian leadership to negotiate seriously and change their calculations, by bolstering the weak position of Croatia. Although this does not necessarily imply an ability to control the Serbian irregulars, it could at least have given impetus to the European Community's peace-making efforts without necessitating the deployment of ground troops.

CONCLUSION

The purpose of this treatment of the Yugoslav crisis is to illustrate four concluding points about the British approach to European security in the post-Thatcher period. The first is a strict belief that there are zones of security/insecurity in Europe, with the fundamental fault-line running (almost) down the old East–West dividing line. Western Europe is a zone of security; the east of the continent has to endure varying degrees of insecurity. Further, there is almost nothing that western Europe can do to improve security relations in those regions. Certainly aid and technical advice can help to alleviate some of the social and economic trauma of the transition to democracy and a market economy; but even *management* of the crises that will be induced by the most pressing security challenges – enduring ethnic unrest – is believed to be beyond the capability of western Europe. And, of course, how much more thankless the task – should it be required – in the former Soviet Union.

The second theme is that if the region of Europe outside NATO is seen firmly to be out-of-area, security within western Europe can only be enhanced on an intergovernmental basis. There is little to be said in favour of a common European Community defence policy. Indeed, the limits of European Community influence have been shown in the Yugoslav crisis: not in the inability to broker even a cease-fire, let alone a peace, but in the inability of the nations of the Community to agree on a course of action. The differing views of each country cannot, it is argued, be subsumed into one overarching policy; and the introduction of majority voting on the subject would be a recipe for tearing the European Community itself apart.

The third theme is drawn from the second. Intergovernmentalism is vital in west European security not only for the above reasons, but also because of the vital importance of continued co-operation with the United States. Euro-enthusiasts, it is felt, exaggerate the capabilities of the west European countries and underestimate those of the United States. Would it be possible, for example, to impose an air exclusion zone over Croatia without the assistance of the United States in terms of its surveillance assets?

The final theme is that on all these points and issues, there is now a consensus in the United Kingdom between the major parties. Of course, there are still differences of nuance on some issues, but these are often designed for internal consumption, and bear little relevance to the subject under discussion. In general, this has had the effect of reducing the salience of the security debate in party political terms, which, in turn, has reduced the level of public discussion on security matters in the United Kingdom. Even the traumas of Yugoslavia have created no real debate or discussion.

The nature of the debate over security in the United Kingdom has thus moved through some subtle changes in the period since November 1990 when John Major became Prime Minister. Much of the bitterness between the Conservative and the Labour Party over the issue of security has disappeared, and the rebuilding of consensus has been marked.[11] But one of the features of that consensus has been a marked unwillingness to move dramatically forward towards a common foreign and security policy by the European Community states, an issue that can only remain a difficult one for Britain in its relationship with its European partners. British conceptions of security still revolve very much around coupling with the United States; it is to be expected that this is the area that British governments of whatever political persuasion will place emphasis on over the next few years.

Much of the research for this article was conducted through off-the-record interviews with officials in London, for which the author would like to express his appreciation.

NOTES

1. For an examination of that debate see for example, Roger Ruston, *A Say in the End of the World* (Oxford: Clarendon Press, 1989).
2. This is not to argue that there is not a difference over foreign policy outlooks; it was, after all, such a difference that in part underlay the choice between Thatcher and Heseltine for the leadership of the Conservative Party. On the broader perspectives see, for example, William Wallace, 'Foreign Policy and National Identity in the United Kingdom', *International Affairs*, Vol.67, No.1, January 1991.
3. For an earlier examination of this view, see Stuart Croft, 'La question Européenne dans la Politique de Securité Britannique', *Politique Etrangère*, No. 1, 1991. On the general themes, see Stuart Croft (ed.) *British Security Policy* (London: Harper Collins, 1991).
4. For an examination of policy under the Thatcher administrations see, for example, Peter Byrd, *British Foreign Policy under Thatcher* (Oxford: Philip Allan, 1988), and John Baylis, *British Defence Policy* (London: Macmillan, 1989).
5. See, for example, Hella Pick, 'Thatcher Still Working for Slowdown of Unification' *The Guardian*, 19 February 1990, and Michael Evans, 'Kohl Aims to Heal German Unity Rift with Thatcher', *The Times*, 26 March 1990. For a collection of useful speeches, see Lawrence Freedman (ed.), *Europe Transformed: Documents on the End of the Cold War* (London: Tri-Service Press, 1990).
6. See, for example, William Wallace, 'Joy Leaves Heartache in London and Paris', *The Guardian*, 4 October 1990.
7. See Michael Brenner, 'The Alliance: a Gulf Post-Mortem', *International Affairs*, Vol.67, No.4, October 1991 on this.
8. On many of these issues and themes, see Mark Hoffman (ed.), *UK Arms Control in the 1990s* (Manchester University Press, 1990).
9. See Helen Wallace, 'The Europe That Came in from the Cold', *International Affairs*, Vol.67, No.4, October 1991 for a general discussion of these issues.
10. On these points, see Dan Keohane, 'Britain's Security Policy and NATO in the 1990s', *Arms Control*, Vol.12, No.1, 1991.
11. On the subject of the recreation of consensus between the parties on foreign and defence policy specifically, and more generally in other areas of policy, see M. Smith and J. Spear (eds.), *The Labour Party in Transition* (London: Routledge, 1992).

The United States, Germany and the New World Order

STEPHEN F. SZABO

A NEW GRAND DEBATE

It is an old maxim of diplomacy that the solution of problems creates new ones. The end of the cold war and the way it ended represent a triumph for Western statecraft and strategy, and yet pose new challenges and the necessity for a fundamental re-examination of basic assumptions and strategy. As the West faces a 'Europe whole and free', in President Bush's phrase, and the end of the Soviet Union as it has existed since the Russian Revolution of 1917, it also begins a new Grand Debate similar in scope to that conducted in the late 1940s when the last new world order was shaped.

The new Grand Debate in the United States, which began with the fall of the Berlin Wall, has been entered fully with the end of Communism in the USSR and the dissolution of the Soviet Union following the failure of August 1991 coup. At issue once again is the kind of international role America should play in a world which no longer faces the Soviet military, ideological and political threat. The key question in the debate is: should the United States continue to play the kind of international role it has done during the cold war, as the leading global power, or rather should it turn more of its attention to domestic concerns and pay less attention to and have a smaller role in international affairs, especially in the security area?

That the world is no longer bipolar is not at issue. The debate in the USA rather, is over whether it is unipolar or multipolar. Those like Charles Krauthammer and other neo-conservatives would argue that we now live in a unipolar age dominated by the only global superpower, the United States, which should use this opportunity to reshape the global order in its own image.[1]

Others, like Robert Hormats, would contend that we have passed into a multipolar world in which economic power will be the foundation for international influence, and that the United States is falling behind the European Community and Japan in key sectors of economic and technological competition.[2] In order to play a leading international role the United States must turn its attention to the task of rebuilding the economic and social bases of economic power at home. Beyond this broad question lie more specific ones, such as against whom does the United States now need to defend itself? How is it to deal with the emerging regional powers of Japan and Germany?

Much of this new Grand Debate will centre on Europe and the future US role on the continent. The cold war ended in Europe and the most significant implications of its termination will be felt on the continent and in US–European relations. US foreign and defence policy has been eurocentric at least since the end of World War II. The largest numbers of American military forces stationed abroad are in Europe, and NATO/Europe has received top priority in terms of American defence planning and spending. Thus the changes which are sweeping through Europe augur equally sweeping changes in the US view and role in that region.

This chapter will briefly look at how a new Europe fits into the Bush administration's view of the 'New World Order' and then will turn to the expectations in the United States over the role of a united Germany in it.

THE NEW ATLANTICISM

In many respects the Europe which has been emerging since the end of the continental division of 1945–1990 is one compatible with the American vision for a new Europe at the end of the 1940s: a post-national Europe organized along the lines of democratic and mixed economy principles and closely linked to the United States. This Europe, it was hoped, would avoid the recurrent crises of nationalism which have pulled the USA into two wars in this century on the continent, while allowing for the United States to remain engaged at an acceptable cost.

American policy makers began to sense the possibilities for a new Europe even before the revolutions of 1989, but the growing prospect of German unification was perhaps the most important impulse in American thinking. President Bush and Secretary of State Baker were sensitive to the mounting criticism in the USA that they were not responding adequately to the dramatic changes in the USSR and eastern Europe. They had, in addition, recognized by the NATO summit in May 1989 that Germany was now the key power in Europe, and that the process of European integration had to be supported as a means of channelling this power in a constructive and non-nationalist direction. Bush had spoken then of the German–American relationship as one of 'partners in leadership'.

This theme was reinvoked as a 'new Atlanticism' at the NATO summit in early December, following the Malta summit. As one American commentator had observed at the time, 'Bush's meaning was clear to those attending the NATO summit: Britain and Margaret Thatcher will play a less significant role in Bush's new alliance architecture. West Germany and the European Community will now be central to America's political and security calculations in Europe.'³ The developments in East Germany provided an urgent impetus to this policy and pushed Bush and Baker toward actively shaping change in the postwar structure of Europe. To the American administration the question of German unification was, as it had been in the immediate postwar period, less important than the creation of a new European order.

This new policy was spelled out first by the President in his meeting with Chancellor Kohl after the December 1989 Soviet–American Malta summit in four principles regarding German unification. These were: (*a*) that the principle of self-determination be respected; (*b*) that it occur as part of a broader process of European integration which included NATO and the EC; (*c*) that it be gradual and peaceful and regarded the interests of other Europeans; and (*d*) that it should occur with respect for the inviolability of borders as stated in the Helsinki Final Act. It was during this meeting that President Bush informed the Chancellor of the American commitment to support German unification fully. From this point on the West Germans were confident of the backing of the United States.

The four principles were further articulated by Baker in his West Berlin speech on 12 December 1989. In it Baker argued that the end of the division of Europe meant that a new architecture was needed for a new era and that this new structure must accomplish two main purposes. First, there must be 'an opportunity to overcome through peace and freedom the division of Berlin and of Germany.' Second , 'the architecture should reflect that America's security – politically, militarily and economically – remains linked to Europe's security.'⁴

The new Atlanticism required new missions for NATO, including a shift in the Alliance toward arms control and other co-operative structures in Europe and closer Alliance co-operation on regional conflicts. Both the Conference on Security and Co-operation in Europe (CSCE) and the EC could play valuable roles in this new architecture. Baker in his speech strongly supported the process of European economic and political integration and proposed a closer US–EC relationship in the future. Yet NATO, and the leading American role it implied, remained fundamental to American thinking about the future new Europe.

By the middle of 1990 the theme of a new Atlanticism and of a 'Europe whole and free' became merged as a building block of the President's New World Order. Bush and Baker saw the emerging new European order as a model for a global order and the *Paris Charter for a New Europe*, signed in November 1990, linked the creation of a more co-operative security structure in Europe to more effective global co-operation in the United Nations.[5]

Yet as the new Europe emerged in the post-unification period, American doubts about an independent Europe also resurfaced. A series of signals sent by the Bush administration to Europe in 1991 including the so called 'Dobbins *démarche*' of February and a speech by Robert Zoellick to the Atlantik Brücke conference, in Berlin in April, raised serious concerns about the movement toward a European security identity.

The main lines of these concerns centred around the development of the Western European Union (WEU) as a security institution of the EC. The administration became worried that a European regional bloc was emerging both in the trade and the security area and that this bloc would become a rival rather than a partner (or subordinate) of the United States.[6] Worries about post-1992 EC as 'Fortress Europe' were rekindled by the failure to reach agreement in the Uruguay round of the GATT negotiations in December. Reservations about a more independent EC organized on security issues were fanned by the Kohl–Mitterrand paper of 4 February, in which the two leaders announced their intention to create a European security community via the WEU.[7] Gorbachev's shift to the 'right' and the increased influence of the KGB and the military on his policies reawakened the administration's caution about the stability of European security. Finally Germany's indecisive global role following unification and Europe's lack of a common response to the Gulf War also opened questions in Washington about the viability of the new Atlanticism.

The possible development of the WEU as a separate European pillar rather than as a bridge to NATO is viewed in Washington as risking the marginalization of NATO and therefore of the American leadership role in Europe. This type of WEU would facilitate European bloc-building against American positions and foster a decoupling of the United States from the Europe of the Community in the security field, a process which could be accelerated by trade disputes and rising European protectionism. The selection of Edith Cresson as French Premier only increased these anxieties.

This possible decoupling is viewed within the administration as dangerous, not only because it risks encouraging neo-isolationism in America, but because it raises the prospect that the United States will face a European rival rather than a partner in the Middle East as well. The Dobbins *démarche* also pointed to the problems a WEU–NATO rivalry could cause in eastern Europe, especially the idea that the EC could intervene militarily in this region. 'It would be a mistake to create the impression that the United States is less interested in the security of eastern Europe than WEU member states . . . The further one goes in this direction, the more one accentuates the security and defence policy separation of Europe and the United States.'[8]

This redefinition by the administration of the new Atlanticism and a reassertion of the claim to American leadership in shaping the new global order was part of a new American self-confidence in the wake of the Gulf War. Although the administration would not endorse more extreme visions of unipolarism, its vision of the New World Order has always emphasized the leading role of the United States.[9]

The failure of the Soviet coup and the rapid collapse of the Soviet Union as an integrated nation-state further upset the administration's calculations. The New World Order was based on the premise of a co-operative relationship with the Soviet Union. With the future of the USSR in serious doubt not only was this assumption placed in question, but so also has the future of the United States' position in Europe.

AMERICAN VIEWS OF THE NEW GERMANY

As the administration has begun to have second thoughts about an independent Europe, it has also been forced to rethink what it wants and can expect from a united Germany. During the early phase of German reunification two broad views of the new Germany's role in the new Europe emerged.

One view, propounded by critics of reunification, was of a 'Bismarckian Germany' which would pursue a strategy of manoeuvre in central Europe designed to enhance Germany's influence at the expense of stability there. Some who held this view feared that the new Germany would weaken its ties to the West and move closer to Moscow in some sort of new Rapallo, that is, a Soviet–German understanding at the expense of the West. Others were more worried about Germany's turning the newly independent eastern European countries into 'economic satellites' and becoming the new hegemon of Europe. In either version, the new Germany would no longer be a vital part of either the Europe Community or the trans-atlantic partnership.

A second view, designed with the first in mind, was the Bush administration's 'partners in leadership' concept. This version saw a more influential Germany as a pillar of the New World Order, bolstering NATO and the European Community while taking on new global responsibilities. As the term implies, this view foresaw a more co-equal

US–German relationship, but not necessarily co-leadership. President Bush was saying to the Germans that they have a responsibility and that he would count on them for leadership.

Neither view has turned out to be correct. In the immediate wake of unification an inward-looking Germany emerged, a Germany which seemed to see itself as a larger version of Switzerland. Internal and external developments worked together to produce a more parochial nation, one which was preoccupied with its own problems of reunification and passionately desiring to be left out of distasteful international involvements.

The administration was disappointed with the level of support it received from Germany during the Gulf War and with Germany's support of what it saw as French protectionist designs in the failure of the GATT Uruguay round in December 1990. It also saw a divergence emerge between its policies toward the Soviet Union and those of the Kohl government.

Yet the leading role taken by the Federal Republic both in the Yugoslav crisis and in extending recognition to the Baltic states has made it clear that, much as it might prefer not to, Germany is being forced into taking a leadership position in the new Europe and the larger emerging global order. What does the United States expect from this new Germany in the key issue areas?

GERMANY AND THE UNITED STATES

The administration looks at the new Germany and asks if the special relationship between the United States and Germany, which already had begun in the 1970s, will remain important to a united Germany? Will the two nations become partners in leadership? Certainly Germany's ability to master the formidable challenges it faces in Europe and beyond will depend on how it manages its key international relationships, with none more key than that with the United States. Washington's strong and unqualified support for unification produced the best German–American relationship since the 1960s. But it is far from clear that this new atmosphere can be translated into a stronger relationship over the longer term.

The points of potential friction are numerous. One is the future of the European security architecture. The United States still continues to view NATO as the primary institution for maintaining order in Europe and for justifying the presence of American forces there. While Germany will want to maintain some American presence and will preserve its membership in NATO, there is likely to be a strong German emphasis upon subordinating the Alliance to a more political pan-European structure, like the CSCE. The Germans will also remain sensitive to French desires to create a more independent European defence identity. The Bush administration, as already noted, while initially supportive of a more European defence identity, seems to have had second thoughts, fearing that this could marginalize American influence in the new Europe and risk leaving a security vacuum if this European identity falters.

The events in the wake of the Soviet coup only raise again doubts about the future of NATO. While the adminstration was confident before the coup that it had stabilized NATO through the terms of German unification, serious questions re-emerged afterwards about the justification for NATO's existence and for a large American military presence in Europe with a much more decentralized Soviet Union.[10]

A German–American debate over the focus and organization of European security seems difficult to avoid. So too does one over the US troop presence and the modernization of nuclear weapons in Germany. With ex-Soviet forces leaving Germany, with the break-up of the Red Army a real possibility, with the new sense of German sovereignty and the pressures on the American defence budget at home, the idea of stationing large numbers of American troops and nuclear weapons on German soil will seem anachronistic if not dangerous to many on both ends of the political spectrum in both the United States and Germany. Yet the removal or erosion of this security link would remove an important pillar of the German–American partnership.

The United States and Germany have demonstrated remarkable flexibility and political sensitivity in rapidly adjusting to new circumstances in Europe. The historic London NATO summit of July 1990 and the NATO strategy review are evidence of this flexibility and of the American realization of the altered strategic environment in Europe. Yet the 1990s will test the statesmanship of Germans and Americans, among others, even more than did the turning point years of 1989 and 1990.

Relations could also be strained by differing American and German attitudes toward the Commonwealth of Independent States (CIS) and the proper policies to pursue. A serious gap between the two sides opened up in the early to mid-1980s over the broad conception of *détente* and relations with the USSR. Since the late 1980s American and German policies toward the Soviet Union have been compatible; however, a new gap threatens to open again. While the United States and Germany were agreed on the broad outlines of how to deal with the USSR and with Gorbachev, divergences were apparent even before the attempted Soviet coup and the unravelling of the Soviet Union which followed. The German stake in a stable CIS is greater and more immediate than that of the USA and is being defined in somewhat different ways which could lead to important policy differences in the future. Already on the general policy of Western assistance to the CIS, the Germans are willing to offer more support without conditions while the Americans prefer to hold up aid until reforms have taken place.

In the wake of the weakening, if not collapse, of the former Soviet Union as an international actor, the Germans are bound to be pulled even more into the vacuum created in central Europe, a vacuum which the United States is unlikely to fill. This has already raised some fringe concerns in the American media over a more dominant Germany which will emerge as a rival to the United States for leadership in the new Europe.[11] A new divergence on policy towards the CIS could further erode the close German–American relationship and thus a co-ordinated German–American approach in this unstable region is vital.

Economic differences could also either exacerbate frictions or, if properly resolved, lead to a new and more stable economic order. During the 1980s the two nations pursued similar strategies on trade and economic growth – fighting inflation and resisting protectionism. Yet the open economic order is threatened both in Europe and globally. A failure of the Uruguay Round would be a disaster for everyone concerned. Beyond GATT fundamental differences seem to be emerging between European and American views on industrial policy. The Europeans believe that they cannot afford to let happen to them what the Americans have permitted to happen in the USA, namely the opening of key industrial and technological sectors to Japan. They wish to avoid a 'hollowing out' of key sectors by protecting core skills and jobs in such vital areas as engineering and computer technology. The Americans, on the other hand, want access to these sectors in post-1992 Europe and fear that attempts to block the Japanese will harm American interests as well. The Germans will be crucial here, as America will expect Germany to keep Europe open.

The 1990s will be, therefore, a time not only for creating a new security architecture but an economic one as well. Less dependent upon the United States for security than during the cold war, Germany may be less inclined to ease frictions over trade, monetary and other economic issues or to support American actions outside Europe. If this turns out to be the case then 'partners in leadership' will be a very empty phrase. Yet a creative response would do much to lead to a prosperous and stable new world order.

William Odom has noted that Europe has been stable when German–

American relations have been close and unstable when these two nations diverge.[12] Given the momentous changes occurring in Europe and in the former USSR, the old German–American partnership will have to adjust to new circumstances in order to be sustained. Continuity is only possible through change.

The United States will have to take the term 'partners' seriously if it really wants to be a partner in leadership. Germany will not be dependent upon the United States for its security to the same degree that West Germany was and will therefore have less interest in supporting American policies and leadership. It needs the Americans less and is more of an equal in the economic and political areas of central importance to the new global order. Not only the unipolarists in the United States will find this hard to accept. The leadership of the United States, if not the public, will find the psychological requirements of adjustment to be more difficult than they perhaps expect. For four decades Americans have been accustomed to playing a hegemonic role. Now they will be in some key ways equals or at least only equally influential. Resentments may emerge about the new German role in this process of adjustment. American official attitudes about a more independent Europe (and Germany) reflect this ambivalence. Complaints about burden-sharing and European 'free riders' can change to concern about European competitors. There will be the mix of admiration and envy which accompanies the success of a former protégé.

The New World Order, if it is to be better than the cold war order, will depend on partnership and co-management of global issues between the United States, Japan and the European Community (with Germany playing a leading role). This new trilateral world will either create an interdependent and open global system, which will benefit the South as well, or it will produce new regional blocs which could lead to increased competition and possible instability.

The German–American relationship will be crucial to the outcome of this process. It will require an adjustment of roles and national self-images which will not be easy for either partner. For the Germans it means their taking on a willingness to lead despite the legacy of a past which makes this difficult both in terms of the German political culture and of the reactions of its neighbours. For the Americans it means the realization that to expect German leadership will mean for them to have to accept more partnership. The USA may be 'bound to lead' but it can no longer do so in the old style. This task of readjustment, however, comes after 40 years of close alliance and friendship, a legacy which provides optimism that both nations are up to the new challenges of 'partners in leadership'.

NOTES

1. Charles Krauthammer, 'Bless Our *Pax Americana*', *Washington Post*, 22 March 1991, p.A25.
2. Robert Hormats, 'The Roots of American Power', *Foreign Affairs*, Vol.70, Summer 1991, pp.132–49.
3. Jim Hoagland, 'The End of the Special Relationship', *Washington Post*, 7 December 1989, p.A27.
4. 'A New Europe, a New Atlanticism: Architecture for a New Era', *Current Policy* (Washington: US Department of State, 1989), No.1233, p.5.
5. See Stanley R. Sloan, 'The US Role in a New World Order: Prospects for George Bush's Global Vision', *CRS Report for Congress* (Washington: Congressional Research Service, Library of Congress, 28 March 1991), p.11.
6. Jim Hoagland, 'Europe – a Great Idea, Up to a Point', *Washington Post*, 25 April 1991, p.A15.
7. 'Amerika befuarchtet seine Ausgrenzung: Bedenken gegen die europauische Sichersheitspolitik', *Frankfurter Allgemeine Zeitung*, 9 April 1991.
8. Quoted in note 7.
9. Note 5, pp.14, 22–23.
10. See, for example, Andrew Rosenthal, 'Farewell, Red Menace', *New York Times*, 1 September 1991, p.A1.
11. See, for example, Rowland Evans and Robert Novak, 'Here Come the Germans', *Washington Post*, 30 August 1991, p.A22.
12. William E. Odom, 'Germany, American and the Strategic Reconfiguration of Europe', in Gary Geipel (ed.), *The Future of Germany* (Indianapolis: Hudson Institute, 1990), pp.190–217.

Implications for the United States

LAWRENCE S. KAPLAN

Europeans have expressed an enduring concern over the past 40 years about the depth of the United States' conversion from its isolationist tradition. The French have been the most eloquent sceptics, declaiming in de Gaulle's time and afterwards that it was illogical for any nation to commit its fortunes and its manpower to the service of another continent. Eventually it will tire of the enterprise and return home. That circumstance would be hastened if its homeland was threatened, as was possible after the Soviets acquired intercontinental ballistic missiles, or if Europeans were not grateful enough for America's services, as was apparent during the Vietnam War. This was the benign French view. If America did continue its involvement in Europe, a darker interpretation would explain American allegiance to NATO as a species of American imperialist control.

But it is not only Frenchmen who doubted the reliability of the American partner. Friends of America inside NATO have wondered from time to time how Americans would react to repeated anti-American behaviour in Europe. Demonstrations against the American presence have periodically marred the relationship. At the peak of the movement against the deployment of cruise and *Pershing* II missiles in Europe a number of NATO officials attending a conference in Bellagio, co-sponsored by the Lemnitzer Center for NATO Studies and the Centro Studia sulla Difesa of the University of Genoa, made clear their dismay at European attitudes towards their major partner, and speculated about their impact on the American public, particularly on college youth. I received a request that the Lemnitzer Center be a *pied-à-terre* for a host of NATO officials who would radiate from Ohio throughout the country to spread the word among the colleges that Europe was not anti-American, that the demonstrators represented a small minority, and that NATO was a vital part of the security of every member. I was a little taken aback by the heat of their argument. While my response was positive, of course, I hesitantly suggested that I was not much aware of a ground swell of resentment in the American colleges, and certainly not at Kent State University, that would justify such an urgent tour. Was American resentment at the demonstrations at Greenham Common touching off demands that the United States should withdraw from Europe? Were we witnessing a neo-isolationism fuelled by European hostility and ingratitude?

The question came up again a little over a year later, after the deployment of the missiles had begun, and after the strength of the anti-nuclear campaign had waned in Europe. The issue was a Senate proposal in June 1984, offered by Senator Sam Nunn to reduce drastically America's contribution to NATO over a period of years if Europeans did not take up their fair share of the burden. There was nothing novel in the proposal; it had none of the passion found in similar Mansfield motions of the late 1960s and early 1970s. American resentment over the putative unfairness of burden-sharing had been periodically manifested since McNamara became exercised over the dollar drain in the balance of payments during the Kennedy administration. What was different was that the sponsor was Senator Nunn, not only a powerful figure in the Senate but a well-known friend of NATO. If Nunn spoke out against Europe, what fate was in store for the Alliance? The Nunn proposal was never put to the test; it was reworded with the help of Senator Cohen and ended up as a toothless warning asking that Europeans should do more than they had in the past. The issue received modest attention in *The New York Times* as a one-day phenomenon; it never reached the *Kent-Ravenna-Record-Courier* on any day.

I mention this would-be crisis because Europeans took it seriously. Foreign Minister Genscher rushed to Washington to assure the State Department and the White House that Europe was doing its share, that it would do even more, and that the threat of an American defection was a frightening prospect for all Europeans. But in fact no such threat existed, and very little attention was paid to it in the press and the country. The circumstances are still not clear. Conceivably, this was an administration ploy to extract more support from the NATO partners, without intending any immediate consequences.

Nunn's initiative disappeared with scarcely a trace in the United States but not in Europe. I can say ruefully that I discovered the Nunn affair in September of that year, in the course of a USIA lecture tour in the Low Countries and Scandinavia. It seemed that everywhere I travelled I would have questions either about why the presidential candidates were not speaking about NATO or why Senator Nunn did speak out. I felt I could answer the first question, but had difficulty with the second. I do read both *The New York Times* and the *Kent-Ravenna-Record-Courier*, but I must have missed *The Times* on the day in June when Nunn unveiled his resolution. I asked the Embassy in Brussels for help, read the text of the resolution, and came up with the same answers I gave to my NATO friends in Italy the year before.

In essence, there has been little or no reaction to various alarms which have agitated the Alliance over the past generation. It is not that the idea of fair distribution of burdens lacks resonance. It does. Periodically, a member of Congress, such as Pat Schroeder, will speak to the subject; others will decry the ingratitude of allies who let Americans continue to carry the major responsibilities of the Alliance, particularly the financial responsibilities, when most of Europe has achieved a standard of living equal to if not superior to that of the United States. But one may question whether this was a resurgence of isolationism, or part of a special agenda. Schroeder, for example, is using NATO as an example of the wastefulness of the military establishment at a time when funds might be used to better advantage elsewhere.

The response I find is not antipathy toward NATO but apathy toward Europe as a given. Apathy is a part of the relationship with the outside world accepted with as much certainty by the youth of this generation as the abstention from European quarrels had been the norm in the century and a half between the termination of the Franco-American alliance of 1778 and the signing of the North Atlantic Treaty.

The NATO team did not gather sufficient funds to make its tour in 1983. Had they done so, they might have been disappointed as well as relieved. The reasons for relief are obvious; they would have found no great ground swell of revulsion against Europe for opposing deployment of American missiles. But they might have been disappointed over the relative disinterest in European affairs, or even knowledge about the Alliance. Again from experience, my classes during the Vietnam War were filled to capacity, if only to vent feelings about reactionary teachers of diplomatic history who had been co-opted by the Establishment. NATO was not at the centre of their concern, but at least the organization was visible at the time, as 'the rather elaborate apparatus', as David Calleo once put it, 'by which we have chosen to organize the American protectorate in Europe'. In the mid-1980s my classes were much smaller, with its chairs occupied by students specializing in international affairs and without notable passions of any kind. In some ways I miss the excitement of the last generation. But I also recognize that apathy or ignorance need not be equated with rejection. Without much exaggeration one may conclude that acceptance of an entangling alliance with Europe was as much a part of the American landscape in the 1980s as was the rejection of secession in the wake of the Civil War in the nineteenth century.

If this judgement is accurate it offers an answer to Europeans who worried in 1984, and perhaps again in 1988, about the absence of NATO in the presidential campaign. Iran and the Middle East were live issues, as were Nicaragua and Latin America, but not Europe. The reason was simply that there was a consensus in both parties that Europe and isolationism were beyond dispute. The nation had embraced the Atlantic community without having to articulate the relationship. Unlike Nicaragua or Iran, there was no one to argue the case to disengage from the Alliance.

Conceivably, the dramatic events of the last two years may make most of the foregoing comments irrelevant. But I have not so far spoken of the menace of Soviet Communism as the inspiration for the sea change in American opinion, and perhaps the glue that has kept the Atlantic community together over the past 40 years. If this was the case, the dissolution of the Warsaw Pact and the crumbling of the Soviet empire may make NATO unnecessary, and may permit the United States to return to the tradition that characterized all of the nineteenth century and almost half of the twentieth.

A return to non-entanglement, however, requires scenarios which are unlikely to become reality. One of them is a world like that of the nineteenth century, in which America would be inviolate no matter what went on on the other side of America's oceans. The internecine quarrels of Europeans, and even the imperialistic thrusts of Europeans into other continents, had little relevance to America's security. There was a sense of the possibility of autarchy, even when the American economy was infused with British money and the outside world with American agricultural products. Such is not the situation in the late twentieth century. Technology may not have made a peaceful world but it has made independence economically and militarily an impossibility. The links to Europe forged over the last half century will be too strong to break, no matter how distressed Americans may be with the way Europeans are organizing their policies and economies.

In a new world order in which the United Nations could play the role of peacekeeper, as originally intended in 1944, there should be no need for NATO. But what are the prospects for an end of national conflicts and with it the end of alliances? They are not bright. In fact, the demise of the Warsaw Pact and the disintegration of the Soviet Union may mean victory in the cold war, but its legacy could mean less security, rather than more for western Europeans. There are at least three elements in any prognosis for Europe to keep the Atlantic Alliance alive. Their order of importance will vary with the fast-changing international scene.

They are, first, the unification of Germany, completed in 1990, and understandably celebrated by all in the West. And for good reason. The Germany of 1991 is a democracy. It has proved itself over the past generation as firmly rooted in the Western tradition as any other ally. If NATO dissolved and the United States withdrew from Europe there would be no imminent sense of danger of a neo-Nazi or irredentist revival in the united Germany. Germany seems to have made its peace with its neighbours and with itself, and should be ready as a responsible democracy to lead a unified Europe, without an American presence on the continent. Nevertheless, there are problems which are inescapable. They centre on such questions as: where would a united Germany take Europe? Its economic power could be mobilized in directions the European Community may not wish to go. And Germany would have the muscle to make its will felt. Economic power can be just as disconcerting as military power. At the base of the misgivings lies an historical memory among Europeans. Will the ghosts of the past revive, particularly if there should be an economic downturn? So while Europeans publicly – and usually sincerely – cheered the fall of the Wall, there is the sense that NATO provides a place for the United States to live alongside Germany, as a comforting balance to calm nervous Europeans. Such was the feeling I had a year ago in touring Italian universities and international centres. Publicly they hailed the prospect that the European Community would become a political as well as an economic entity; privately, I was told that an American evacuation of Europe would be a psychological disaster. The United States still has a role to play in Europe.

If a latent concern about Germany still animates Europeans, the spectre of anarchy, civil war, and ethnic conflict in eastern Europe and the Commonwealth of Independent States (CIS) is much more disturbing as a problem for the immediate future. The pride which the West feels in the dissolution of the Warsaw Pact and in the movements toward capitalism and democracy in what had been the Second World has to be qualified by the new Balkan wars already in process in Yugoslavia, with potential replication in other ethnically divided nations of eastern Europe. Liberation from the Communist yoke need not bring democracy; it could bring nationalism, xenophobia, and fascism in its wake. The breakdowns in eastern Europe could touch the vital interests of western Europeans.

If this is a disturbing prognosis for eastern Europe, the future of a dissolved Soviet Union is even more sobering. Not only might there be civil war in the future, but an economic disaster that could bring to power a military dictatorship with expansionist ambitions is also possible. The West cannot forget that its present weakness notwithstanding, the CIS is still a superpower militarily. Not even the fast pace of demilitarization would affect the potential for mass destruction if its nuclear power should fall into the hands of radical leaders. In this context NATO's more modest military forces will not be permitted to disband. And while the United States' share of the troops will continue to decline rapidly, its nuclear shield remains in place for more than psychological reasons. Although the Warsaw Pact has disappeared, it is an illusion to believe that, with the end of the cold war, NATO has been deprived of any military mission in Europe.

The recent war in the Persian Gulf dramatized a third area of NATO activity, in which the United States has a continuing and probably paramount role to play. With all the talk of a rapid deployment corps composed primarily of the European members of NATO, only the United States has the infrastructure to make it effective in the event of new crises 'out of area'. For most of its history 'out of area' has been the most intractable of NATO's internal quarrels, repeatedly ending in frustration. Witness the problems the Suez crisis in 1956, Vietnam in the 1960s, and the Middle East in the 1970s had presented to the Alliance. If a major threat to the West, and particularly to Europe, could come from irresponsible tyrants from the Third World commanding vital resources, 'out of area' and a rapid deployment force may be the focus rather than the periphery of NATO activity.

The foregoing considerations may be irrelevant if a new security entity comes into being, or if an older one takes on new authority. Conceivably the European Community combining with the Western European Union could provide security for Europe and dispense with the presence of NATO. The EC's efforts in Yugoslavia in the summer of 1991 pointed in this direction. More fanciful, perhaps, but still possible would be a consensus that would permit the United Nations to assume the functions which many had hoped for almost half a century ago. If the United Nations could fill this role, NATO could dissolve or become a regional organization within the terms of Article 53 of the Charter.

Regrettably, there is little likelihood that the functions which NATO assumes today will be taken over by other organizations. In brief, there is no substitute for the American presence in NATO, even if the form of the organization is changed and American authority is reduced. It is worth noting that, with all the talk of the end of the Alliance, if not the end of history, not one member nation has taken advantage of Article 13 of the North Atlantic Treaty and denounced the Treaty in preparation for withdrawal. Not one nation has demanded any immediate removal of American troops from Europe. There was more activity on that front in the United States during the Vietnam War or in Europe during the debate on the deployment of cruise and *Pershing* missiles than there is today. At least in the short run there is no alternative to NATO.

Appendix One:
The Western European Union's Role in the Emergence of a New European Security Order[1]

WILLEM VAN EEKELEN

THE NEED FOR A REJUVENATED TRANSATLANTIC SECURITY PARTNERSHIP

In this respect words matter. I prefer to speak of a transatlantic strategic contract and of partnership for its implementation. We should avoid words with commercial overtones when we address security issues. In the economic field, Europe and America are competitors. In the political and the strategic field we are allies with mutual duties and reciprocal responsibilities. The redefinition of the latter is at the core of the Alliance's adaptation to the new context.

America and Western Europe share common values and are linked by a common history of success in deterring war, containing and finally bringing about the demise of Communism. The Alliance must therefore be preserved and modernised.

For the present and the future we can only succeed in promoting stability and defeating war by remaining partners on the basis of our common strategic interests and through the well-oiled mechanisms of wide-ranging political consultations in the North Atlantic Council.

The more the Alliance remains focused on collective defence the easier it will be to maintain and justify a joint effort on both sides of the Atlantic. Collective defence is the core function that will enable NATO consultative and decision-making mechanisms to be kept alive and kicking for all purposes.

By way of introduction I could hardly do better than quote what Frank Carlucci wrote in the preface to a recently published book about the future of NATO in the new Europe. 'We have', I quote, 'seen our most cherished dreams for eastern Europe realized and Communism as a political force is spent. Yet we have been reminded by events in the Middle East – and I should now add in Yugoslavia – that we do not live in a threat-free world. Wherever there is instability, there are risks that even the most sophisticated cannot foresee.'

This diagnosis, which I fully share, is indeed at the root of all European efforts to define a new security order throughout our continent, which appears more fragmented than it ever was. This can only be achieved by beefing-up the existing institutions, the CSCE, NATO and WEU, and by creating the necessary bridges with other European institutions, intergovernmental as well as parliamentary.

I shall focus my remarks on three themes:

- the necessary transatlantic security partnership;
- the reinforcement of European cohesion to face new risks and address conflicting priorities;
- WEU's contribution to stability in the continent of Europe as well as out of Europe.

Recognizing the positive nature of the ongoing development of a European security identity and defence role is the second key element of the Alliance's future vitality.

Although defence is a lower priority for our governments, the new transatlantic contract will not be less binding because it will retain a nuclear as well as a conventional dimension. Active consultation between the three Western nuclear powers is essential in view of the new steps towards the raising of the nuclear threshold in Europe. The nature of security is changing, the threat having been replaced by diffuse and unpredictable risks. Deterrence remains essential, but other dimensions of security are increasing in importance: the export of democracy requires huge investments in economic aid rather than in weaponry.

NATO has a key role to play in the definition of the size and purpose of military forces in the new European context. The mutual commitment requires more innovative co-operation to ensure an adequate level of compatibility between the operational capabilities of American and European forces. A multinational approach should be promoted wherever possible (logistics, procurement, training). There is indeed a real danger of 'renationalization' of defence policies as it becomes harder to apply objective criteria for quantifying the national contributions required for common defence. With the disappearance of the 'layer cake' defence configuration of national sectors along the Iron Curtain, new criteria will have to be developed. The decision to establish a multinational Rapid Reaction Corps (RCC) able to go anywhere in the NATO area is a step in this direction.

Defence will no longer receive the priority it has been given in the past and can no longer exercise a moderating influence on transatlantic relations. Transatlantic relations will at the same time have co-operative and competitive aspects. They will be the fabric of the Alliance's dynamism provided we strive to make harmony prevail. For Americans, NATO is the leading channel for an active role in European affairs; but it cannot be an exclusive channel for transatlantic relations. Organizational parallelism is inevitable. My main conclusion is that NATO's success calls for its rejuvenation on the basis of two pillars. For that reason, European cohesion in security affairs must have both a political and military underpinning. It should receive strong encouragement from the North American allies.

A NECESSARY REINFORCEMENT OF EUROPEAN COHESION

With the Single Act signed in Luxembourg in 1985, the European Community emerged from a period of 'eurosclerosis' centred on the realization of a free internal market; it also provided for closer links between economic policy and foreign policy. Since the ending of the division of Europe, the EC is caught in midstream. The Community is challenged to enlarge its membership: Turkey, Austria and Sweden are candidates. Eastern and central European countries are requesting association agreements, paving the way for future membership. The Community needs a common definition of its future in order to tackle the problems of deepening and enlargement. For that reason, the twin Intergovernmental Conferences on Monetary Union and on Political Union were convened, with the aim of reaching conclusions at the EC Summit meeting at Maastricht in December 1991.

Until 1990, there was little inclination to emphasize Europe's role and capabilities except outside Europe, as was demonstrated by the mine-clearing operations in the Gulf in 1987. That same year, the WEU Platform on European Security Interests stated in its preamble that European integration would remain incomplete without a defence dimension. That awareness grew when the collective defence scenario lost some of its urgency and discussions on a European Political Union highlighted the need for a process of convergence between economic and foreign policy, and ultimately defence aspects as well. Increasingly, the debate centred on the question of whether, and if so how, the Western European Union might become both the European pillar of NATO and the defence dimension of European integration. WEU was described as a 'crossroads organization' or as a 'bridge' between NATO and the future European Union.

WEU is not a perfect pillar in terms of membership. It does not include members of the European Community such as Denmark, Greece and Ireland, nor allies like Norway, Iceland and Turkey. Yet it is the only European pillar available and within the Alliance there is increasing awareness of the need for such a pillar. In Washington, the useful role WEU played 'out-of-area' was recognized. American concern grew, however, when the scope of the discussions was extended to include possible activities in eastern Europe as well. Simultaneously there was talk of a link between WEU and the European Council of Heads of Government, which met two or three times a year to give direction to the European Commuity.

On the eve of the WEU Ministerial meeting which debated European security architecture (on 22 February 1991), diplomatic notes were handed over in capitals to explain US objections to planned WEU activities. These notes were prompted by the 4 February Franco-German proposal in the IGC that WEU should be subordinate to the European Council, thereby developing a European security component solely within the EC that could marginalize NATO. Because the EC was not within the Alliance, subordinating WEU to it could be perceived as accentuating the independence of the European pillar from the Alliance, with the risk of bloc positions being created. The USA accepted that outside Europe there could be a 'distinct and obvious' role for WEU and a different basis for transatlantic collaboration. But WEU should not compete with NATO's missions, nor introduce ambiguity about whether the Alliance in its entirety would stand behind a threatened member wherever the threat might come from.

This *démarche* provided ammunition to those who argued that US support for European integration lasted only up to the moment that Europeans finally took some concrete action. Others emphasized that, to be credible, WEU had to acquire some specifically European operational capabilities.

WEU Ministers decided to publish a paper drafted by the Secretary-General defining the practical steps to be taken with regard to both NATO and EPU. Assuming that the Secretariat would move from London to Brussels, inputs could be made in both directions. WEU members would form a caucus on important items of the respective agendas and, when appropriate, make a joint contribution to NATO consultations. They would not introduce their positions as *faits accomplis* and would consult before decisions were taken.

Another point in the American argument was that the USA did not want to become an 'ally of last resort', called in when Europeans had to be extricated from a problem of their own creation, especially in eastern Europe. Again, Washington's approach seemed to be unduly apprehensive about a perception that the USA might take less interest in the security of eastern Europe than WEU members. Marginalization of the USA by the Europeans is hardly conceivable. In any event, NATO would be engaged in daily consultation, even if the scope for action would be very small. Besides, it is far from certain that Europeans would act if, in the process of consultation, the USA objected to the measures envisaged.

The crux of the matter we all face as allies is the extent to which a European defence identity can be developed which has not only a role outside Europe but also within our continent. The fear has to be overcome in Washington that the further one goes in this direction – even if only in words – the more one would create a gap between Europe and America in the fields of security and defence.

I believe, on the contrary, that a European Union with a defence dimension would closely co-operate with NATO. Until it becomes a reality, Europe can best be an active and reliable partner through the recognition of an operational role for WEU. In two Gulf crises and now in the Yugoslav crisis it has been made clear that such a competence is well deserved, for WEU has established itself as an effective framework for an *ad hoc* co-ordination of European contributions and actions. A WEU with operational responsibilities would be in a position to develop an organic and complementary relationship with the Community and with NATO. I am convinced that WEU would serve the cause of convergence among all the allies rather than justify the fears of those who see it sowing the seeds of divergence.

WEU'S CONCRETE CONTRIBUTION TO COMMON SECURITY AND STABILITY

Let me illustrate this by pointing out the main lessons so far from the Gulf and the Yugoslav conflict from a WEU viewpoint.

The Gulf crisis has exemplified WEU's adaptability and fully justified its reactivation.

The out-of-Europe competence of WEU which is in the Brussels Treaty is a real asset for the Alliance since it offers both a potential for concerted action among Europeans and *ad hoc* co-operation between Europeans and their North American allies.

The scope of WEU military co-ordination has been defined by the Permanent Council in the following terms:

> Co-ordination of the action of armed forces of WEU countries can certainly be envisaged under the auspices of WEU. The operations in the Gulf have set an example of useful co-operation among member states. Nevertheless, the provision of contingents for humanitarian or peacekeeping operations is a matter to be decided nationally by these countries. It is not WEU's responsibility to announce in advance that member states are prepared to co-ordinate such action. Any national decisions to commit forces should be taken with due regard for the overall political context, which is, in fact, a matter for EPC.

When the Security Council ordered the economic and military boycott of Iraq, a major naval effort was undertaken by European nations to enforce economic sanctions and the embargo. The Council met several times in extraordinary session with European NATO and EC countries represented as observers. So did WEU Chiefs of Defence Staff.

The necessary co-ordination mechanisms were expanded. The *ad hoc* group of foreign and defence ministry representatives, which headed a network of naval and military points of contact and had a permanent co-ordination cell in Paris, was its lynchpin. Throughout the crisis, the *ad hoc* group drew up politico-military guidelines which created the framework for liaison among the commands of member states' naval units deployed in areas defined in and around the Gulf.

A WEU 'naval co-ordination authority' was set up on the eve of the beginning of military operations. Each WEU member state took its own decisions on the deployment of forces, in full exercise of its sovereignty. Missions were assigned to those forces by their own governments, to apply the embargo strategy. WEU's field of concertation was subsequently extended to include the definition and implemention of missions, the exchange of information, the definition of action zones, and co-ordination of force deployments, the mutual protection of vessels in the area, and logistic and operational support, all in close co-operation with the American forces on the spot, as well as through Alliance mechanisms. Via the European Community, WEU countries also provided economic aid to the countries in the region more directly affected by the crisis.

As Mr Roland Dumas, the French Foreign Minister and then Chairman of the WEU Council, stated:

> A great step forward has been taken in the quest for common security and common defence . . . this crisis has shown that the WEU countries are capable of coming together, taking joint decisions, giving political guidance and, what is more, translating into action their stated political will.

Consultation on European security problems should be developed on several levels in WEU, particularly in respect of risk assessment, arms control, the monitoring of the proliferation of ballistic, nuclear and chemical weapons, and the regulation of arms exports. Let me give you an example. In the field of verification of arms control agreements, WEU states attach great importance to the 'Open Skies' regime which would help transatlantic cohesion in giving them the possibility to observe military activities in eastern Russia. This would constitute an improvement over the CFE Treaty provisions. Few regions in the world call so urgently for the harmonization of European policies as the Gulf and the Mediterranean. WEU could be the forum for forward thinking about the strategic changes brought about by demographic, social and economic developments.

The crucial importance in the Gulf conflict of intelligence, its gathering and analysis has clearly demonstrated the value to European countries of acquiring an independent satellite observation system which might be operated by a WEU agency, for both the prevention and management of crises. In deciding on 27 June 1991 to set up a satellite data-interpretation centre, WEU Ministers made a significant first step in that direction. The weaknesses of Europe's strategic transport capability is also being tackled.

The Gulf crisis and now the Yugoslav conflict spur WEU member States to develop joint planning and establish joint capabilities. A European arms policy is increasingly needed. A genuine division of labour among Europeans is the only way of combining greater effectiveness and interoperability with the economies of scale and costs made possible by standardization.

The military invasion of Croatia by Serbia and the extraordinary spread of ethnic unrest across eastern Europe, which would lead to more bloodshed, may well do much – in the run-up to the Maastricht Summit – to convince European leaders of the urgent need to endow WEU with the permanent structures it needs to reach joint decisions on continental and out-of-Europe security problems and, where necessary, to effectively apply plans of action tailored to possible theatres of operation.

As regards Yugoslavia, I wonder whether it is appropriate anymore to speak of a civil war. What we have in effect seen since 3 October is a take-over by Serbian Communists and a military invasion of Croatia. In my view, the leaders and commanders involved on the Serbian side are a clique akin to the one which launched the foiled coup in Moscow last August. The UN in their Resolution 713 have commended the European reaction. To intervene in Yugoslavia, Europe needs the blessing of the UN Security Council, the endorsement of the CSCE – responsible for the enforcement of principles and for conflict prevention – and a common Community policy which could finally lead to a mandate for WEU action in the field. The action envisaged – at the stage of pre-contingency planning – is a reinforcement of the observers' mission with the possibility of guaranteeing their security in an autonomous way. Intervention as such or interposition would be on a different scale and probably imply a long-term military commitment. The evolution of the situation may render such a course of action unavoidable, but, so far, the political prerequisites remain: an effective cease-fire and the consent of all parties involved.

The WEU *ad hoc* group has been reactivated and has been engaged in intense work since late September. All the other mechanisms set up at the time of the Gulf crisis could similarly be reactivated at very short notice.

CONCLUDING REMARKS

The debate on the European security identity has given WEU a high profile on the European stage both within the Alliance and in the discussions of the Intergovernmental Conference on Political Union.

Until such time as WEU merges with the European Union, it can play the same contributory role with regard to European political co-operation as described above in relation to NATO. WEU could caucus on items on the European agenda and contribute to their deliberation. Establishing the secretariat in Brussels would make it easier to work with NATO and European institutions. It would also facilitate relations with non-member countries. Within WEU it seems possible to agree on the presence of the other European allies as observers when discussing important matters on the NATO agenda. This happened in ministerial meetings on the Gulf and Yugoslavia.

Two fundamental questions lie at the heart of the matter: 'What is the common vision which Europeans have of their future?', and 'Are the Europeans ready to make the political choice to include the security and defence dimensions in their project for Political Union?' These questions can now be addressed without fearing that a positive answer would lead to a weakening of the Atlantic Alliance. The Copenhagen Ministerial meeting of June 1991 clearly concluded that there was no contradiction between European integration in the security field and the strengthening of solidarity between the 16 signatories of the Washington Treaty.

The Copenhagen communiqué stated that 'the allies that are not currently participating in the development of a European identity in foreign and security policy and defence should be adequately involved in decisions that may affect their security'. Indeed, information mechanisms exist and are currently being expanded to all interested countries. The 14 European members of NATO lack the political framework to provide a European defence identity. WEU brings together countries prepared to go further in defence co-operation, but their relationship with the evolving European Union is still to be defined. Under these circumstances WEU is both the European pillar of NATO and the emerging European defence identity, as there are simply no other possibilities.

Whatever the long-term perspectives for European defence, 1991 offers an historic opportunity to expand WEU's role. Would otherwise a 'common European defence policy' be based on sufficient defence capabilities? Would otherwise the reformed and re-invigorated Alliance still have the necessary dynamism to maintain a viable transatlantic security partnership?

NOTE

1. Paper presented to a Congressional Executive Dialogue on *NATO's Relationship of the Other Instruments of European Security, Washington, DC, 10 October 1991; reprinted with permission.*

Appendix Two:
Declaration of the Member States of the Western European Union Issued on the Occasion of the 46th European Council Meeting on 9 and 10 December 1991 at Maastricht

DECLARATION ON WESTERN EUROPEAN UNION

The Conference notes the following declarations:

I. DECLARATION

of Belgium, Germany, Spain, France, Italy, Luxembourg, the Netherlands, Portugal and the United Kingdom of Great Britain and Northern Ireland, which are members of the Western European Union and also members of the European Union on

THE ROLE OF THE WESTERN EUROPEAN UNION
AND ITS RELATIONS WITH THE EUROPEAN UNION AND
WITH THE ATLANTIC ALLIANCE

Introduction

1. WEU Member States agree on the need to develop a genuine European security and defence identity and a greater European responsibility on defence matters. This identity will be pursued through a gradual process involving successive phases. WEU will form an integral part of the process of the development of the European Union and will enhance its contribution to solidarity within the Atlantic Alliance. WEU Member States agree to strengthen the role of WEU, in the longer term perspective of a common defence policy within the European Union which might in time lead to a common defence, compatible with that of the Atlantic Alliance.
2. WEU will be developed as the defence component of the European Union and as the means to strengthen the European pillar of the Atlantic Alliance. To this end, it will formulate common European defence policy and carry forward its concrete implementation through the further development of its own operational role.

WEU Member States take note of Article J.4 relating to the common foreign and security policy of the treaty on European Union which reads as follows:

1. The common foreign and security policy shall include all questions related to the security of the Union, including the eventual framing of a common defence policy, which might in time lead to a common defence.

2. The Union requests the Western European Union (WEU), which is an integral part of the development of the Union, to elaborate and implement decisions and actions of the Union which have defence implications. The Council shall, in agreement with the institutions of the WEU, adopt the necessary practical arrangements.

3. Issues having defence implications dealt with under this Article shall not be subject to the procedures set out in Article J.3.

4. The policy of the Union in accordance with this Article shall not prejudice the specific character of the security and defence policy of certain Member States and shall respect the obligations of certain Member States under the North Atlantic Treaty and be compatible with the common security and defence policy established within that framework.

5. The provisions of this Article shall not prevent development of closer cooperation between two or more Member States on a bilateral level, in the framework of the WEU and the Atlantic Alliance provided such cooperation does not run counter to or impede that provided for in this Title.

6. With a view to furthering the objective of this Treaty, and having in view the date of 1998 in the context of Article XII of the Brussels Treaty, the provisions of this article may be revised as provided for in Article N (2) on the basis of a report to be presented in 1996 by the Council to the European Council, which shall include an evaluation of the progress made and the experience gained until then.

A. WEU's relations with European Union

3. The objective is to build up WEU in stages as the defence component of the European Union. To this end, WEU is prepared, at the request of the European Union, to elaborate and implement decisions and actions of the Union which have defence implications.

To this end, WEU will take the following measures to develop a close working relationship with the Union:
– as appropriate, synchronization of the dates and venues of meetings and harmonization of working methods;
– establishment of close cooperation between the Council and Secretariat-General of WEU on the one hand, and the Council of the Union and General-Secretariat of the Council on the other;

- consideration of the harmonization of the sequence and duration of the respective Presidencies;
- arranging for appropriate modalities so as to ensure that the Commission of the European Communities is regularly informed and, as appropriate, consulted on WEU activities in accordance with the role of the Commission in the common foreign and security policy as defined in the Treaty on European Union;
- encouragement of closer cooperation between the Parliamentary Assembly of WEU and the European Parliament.

The WEU Council shall, in agreement with the competent bodies of the European Union, adopt the necessary practical arrangements.

B. WEU's relations with the Atlantic Alliance

4. The objective is to develop WEU as a means to strengthen the European pillar of the Atlantic Alliance. Accordingly, WEU is prepared to develop further the close working links between WEU and the Alliance and to strengthen the role, responsibilities and contributions of WEU Member States in the Alliance. This will be undertaken on the basis of the necessary transparency and complementarity between the emerging European security and defence identity and the Alliance. WEU will act in conformity with the positions adopted in the Atlantic Alliance.

- WEU Member States will intensify their coordination on Alliance issues which represent an important common interest with the aim of introducing joint positions agreed in WEU into the process of consultation in the Alliance which will remain the essential forum for consultation among its members and the venue for agreement on policies bearing on the security and defence commitments of Allies under the North Atlantic Treaty.
- Where necessary, dates and venues of meetings will be synchronized and working methods harmonized.
- Close cooperation will be established between the Secretariats-General of WEU and NATO.

C. Operational role of WEU

5. WEU's operational role will be strengthened by examining and defining appropriate missions, structures and means, covering in particular:
- WEU planning cell;
- closer military cooperation complementary to the Alliance, in particular in the fields of logistics, transport, training and strategic surveillance;
- meetings of WEU Chiefs of Defence Staff;

- military units answerable to WEU.

Other proposals will be examined further, including:

- enhanced cooperation in the field of armaments with the aim of creating a European armaments agency;
- development of the WEU Institute into a European Security and Defence Academy.

Arrangements aimed at giving WEU a stronger operational role will be fully compatible with the military dispositions necessary to ensure the collective defence of all Allies.

D. Other measures

6. As a consequence of the measures set out above, and in order to facilitate the strengthening of WEU's role, the seat of the WEU Council and Secretariat will be transferred to Brussels.

7. Representation on the WEU Council must be such that the Council is able to exercise its functions continuously in accordance with Article VIII of the modified Brussels Treaty. Member States may draw on a double-hatting formula, to be worked out, consisting of their representatives to the Alliance and to the European Union.

8. WEU notes that, in accordance with the provisions of Article J.4(6) concerning the common foreign and security policy of the Treaty on European Union, the Union will decide to review the provisions of this Article with a view to furthering the objectives to be set by it in accordance with the procedure defined. The WEU will re-examine the present provisions in 1996. This re-examination will take account of the progress and experience acquired and will extend to relations between WEU and the Atlantic Alliance.

II DECLARATION

of Belgium, Germany, Spain, France, Italy, Luxembourg,
the Netherlands, Portugal and the United Kingdom
of Great Britain and Northern Ireland which are
members of the Western European Union

The Member States of WEU welcome the development of the European security and defence identity. They are determined, taking into account the role of WEU as the defence component of the European Union and as the means to strengthen the European pillar of the Atlantic Alliance, to put the relationship between WEU and the other European States on a new basis for the sake of stability and security in Europe. In this spirit, they propose the following:

States which are members of the European Union are invited to accede to WEU on conditions to be agreed in accordance with Article XI of the modified Brussels Treaty, or to become observers if they so wish. Simultaneously, other European Member States of NATO are invited to become associate members of WEU in a way which will give them the possibility of participating fully in the activities of WEU.

The Member States of WEU assume that treaties and agreements corresponding with the above proposals will be concluded before 31 December 1992.

Notes on Contributors

Stuart Croft is Deputy Director of the Graduate School of International Studies at the University of Birmingham. He is the editor of the journal, *Arms Control: Contemporary Security Policy*, and the book, *British Security Policy* (1991). His articles have appeared in *Politique Etrangère*, *Diplomacy and Statecraft*, *Futures*, *Defense Analysis*, and *International Affairs*, and he has made contributions to numerous edited works. He has delivered papers at a variety of conferences including the International Studies Association Annual Convention, Vancouver, 1991, and the International Political Science Association World Congress, Buenos Aires, 1991, and has addressed conventions in Moscow, Pittsburgh, Calgary, Paris, Stockholm, and Prague. He is currently engaged in compiling *The End of Superpower: British Conceptions of a Changing World, 1945–51*, and the edited volume, *The CFE Treaty*. His next project will be a volume analysing the themes underlying the dramatic changes in the security context of Europe, focusing on the years 1989–92.

Admiral Sir James Eberle GCB LLD became Director of the Royal Institute of International Affairs in January 1984 and retired in December 1990. His first career was in the Royal Navy and in 1976 he became a member of the Admiralty board. He was subsequently appointed Commander-in-Chief Fleet, Allied Commander-in-Chief Channel, NATO Commander-in-Chief Eastern Atlantic, and Commander-in-Chief Naval Home Command. He retired from the Royal Navy in 1983. He takes a particular interest in East–West, especially Anglo–Soviet relations, questions of global security, European defence co-operation, Anglo–Argentine relations, and naval arms control. He has written, lectured and broadcast extensively on many aspects of international affairs.

James E. Goodby is Distinguished Service Professor of International Peace and Security at Carnegie Mellon University. During a 35-year career as a foreign service officer, he was head of the US delegation to the Stockholm Conference on Disarmament in Europe, Vice Chairman of the US delegation to the Strategic Arms Reduction talks (START) and Ambassador to Finalnd. He has written extensively on European Security, peacekeeping, confidence-building measures, and Korea. His publications include 'Peacekeeping in the New Europe', *The*

Washington Quarterly (Spring 1992); 'The New World Order in Northeast Asia', *The Korean Journal of Defense Analysis* (Summer 1991); and 'A New European Concert: Settling Disputes in CSCE', *Arms Control Today* (January 1991).

Lawrence Kaplan is Professor Emeritus, Kent State University, where he was the Director of the University's Lemnitzer Center. Dr Kaplan has written extensively on the history of American diplomacy and foreign policy and on the evolution of United States policy towards NATO. He is author of *The United States and NATO: The Formative Years* (Lexington: University Press of Kentucky, 1984); *A Community of Interests: NATO and the Military Assistance Program, 1948–1951* (Washington: Government Printing Office, 1980); *NATO and the United States: The Enduring Alliance* (Boston: Twayne, 1988), as well as many book chapters and articles on NATO.

Robbin Laird is a Research Staff Member at the Institute for Defense Analysis. He has written extensively on European security, East–West relations, and Soviet foreign and domestic policy. His publications include: *Classic Issues in Soviet Domestic Policy*, with Erik Hoffmann and Fred Fleron (Aldine Press, 1992); *The Soviet Union and Western Europe* (Cambridge University Press, 1992); *The Soviets, Germany and the New Europe* (Westview Press, 1992); *The Europeanization of the Alliance* (Westview Press, 1991); *France, Germany and the Future of the Alliance* (Cambridge University Press, 1990).

Andrei Markovits is an Associate Professor in the Department of Political Science at Boston University and is a Senior Associate at the Center for European Studies at Harvard University. Markovits has a distinguished list of publications on the German Left and German labour unions, including *The Politics of the West German Trade Unions* (Cambridge University Press, 1986) and his forthcoming *The German Left: Red, Green and Beyond* (Cambridge University Press, 1993). He has also had work on related subjects published in a variety of journals including *Comparative Politics*, *German Studies Review*, *German Politics and Society*, *Leviathan*, *New German Critique* and *West European Politics*.

Joseph Pilat is on the staff of the Center for National Security of Los Alamos National Laboratory. He was a special adviser to the Department of Energy's representative of the Secretary of Defense to the 1990 NPT review conference. He also served in 1990 as the

representative of the Secretary of Defense to the Open Skies nego-
tiations. He has been Special Assistant to the Principal Director and
Assistant for Nonproliferation Policy in the Office of the Deputy
Assistant Secretary of Defense for Negotiations Policy. He has been a
Senior Research Associate at the Congressional Research Service, and
has taught at Georgetown University, where has was a Philip E.
Mosely Fellow at the Center for Strategic and International Studies.
He has written widely on defense and national security issues, and is
the editor of *The Non Proliferation Predicament* (Transaction Books,
1985), and co-editor of *Atoms for Peace: An Analysis after Thirty Years*
(Westview Press, 1985); *The Nuclear Suppliers and Nonproliferation:
International Policy Choices* (Lexington Books, 1985), and *Beyond
1995: The Future of the NPT Regime* (Plenum, 1990).

Simon Reich is an Associate Professor in the Graduate School of Public
and International Affairs at the University of Pittsburgh. He has
written extensively on Germany. Included among his publications on
that country are two books: *The Fruits of Fascism: Postwar Prosperity
in Historical Perspective* (Cornell University Press, 1990), and the co-
edited *The New Germany in the New Europe* with Andrei Markovits
and Michael Huelshoff (University of Michigan Press, 1993). Reich
has also published articles on aspects of American trade and investment
policy including 'Roads to Follow: Regulating Foreign Direct Investment' (*International Organization*, Fall 1989). He is presently working
on a co-authored book with Andrei Markovits entitled *Winning with
Grace: Germany in the New Age* (Cornell University Press, 1993).

Jack Snyder is Professor of Political Science at Columbia University. He
is author of *The Ideology of the Offensive: Military Decision Making
and the Disasters of 1914* (Cornell University Press, 1984); *Myths
of Empire: Domestic Politics and International Ambition* (Cornell
University Press, 1991); with Robert Jervis, *Dominoes and Band-
wagons* (Oxford, 1991); and numerous articles on current Soviet
affairs in *International Security*.

James Sperling is Assistant Professor, Department of Political Science at
the University of Akron. Dr Sperling has also taught at Michigan State
University and at Davidson College. He is co-editor of *The Federal
Republic and NATO: Forty Years After* (London: Macmillan, 1991),
has contributed to both *German Studies Review* and Carl Lankowski
(ed.) *Germany and the European Community after the Cold War* (New
York: St Martin's, 1992).

Stephen Szabo is Associate Dean for Academic Affairs at the Paul Nitze School of Advanced International Studies, Johns Hopkins University, Washington, DC. He previously held positions at the National War College and at the Foreign Service Institute. In 1988 he was a fellow at the Woodrow Wilson International Center for Scholars. Dr Szabo is author of *The Changing Politics of German Security* (St Martin's Press, 1990) and editor of *The Bundeswehr and Western Security* (Macmillan, 1989), as well as numerous articles and book chapters on European security.

Willem van Eekelen is Secretary-General of the Western European Union and was formerly Minister of Defence in the Netherlands. Dr van Eekelen has written extensively on European security issues and especially on the role of the Western European Union.

Phil Williams is currently Director of the Ridgway Center, University of Pittsburgh, and Professor of International Security in the Graduate School of Public and International Affairs. During the 1980s, he spent four years at the Royal Institute for International affairs, where he directed projects on Atlantic relations and superpower *détente*, and where in 1988/89 he was Acting Director of the International Security Program. He has written articles on security topics for *Survival*, *International Affairs*, *Washington Quarterly*, and *Defense Nationale*. He is the author of *Crisis Management* (1976), *The Senate and US Troops in Europe* (1986), a co-author of *Superpower Détente* (1988), and has edited or co-edited several books on superpower relations. Dr Williams is currently completing a book entitled *Changing Patterns of Security: From Crisis Prevention to Crisis Management*. He is a consultant to the Institute for Defense Analyses and to the center for National Security Studies, Los Alamos.

Thomas-Durell Young is an Associate Research Professor of National Security Affairs at the Strategic Studies Institute of the US Army War College in Carlisle, Pennsylvania. Dr Young has written extensively on European security issues and is author of 'The Need for NATO-Europe's Substrategic Nuclear Weapons', *Orbis* (Spring 1992). His other publications include: 'Conventional Arms Control and Disarmament: Lessons from the Interwar Period', *Comparative Strategy* (1991); 'Germany, France and the Future of Western European Security', *Parameters* (1990); 'Problems in Australia's Defense Revolution', *Contemporary Southeast Asia* (1989).

Index